THE GLORY

RETURNS TO THE

WORKPLACE

RICHARD FLEMING

DESTINY IMAGE® EUROPE
Via Maiella, 1
66020 San Giovanni Teatino (Ch) - Italy

ISBN 10: 88-89127-04-X
ISBN 13: 978-88-89127-04-9

For Worldwide Distribution. Printed in Italy.

2 3 4 5 6 7 8 / 10 09 08 07 06

This book and all other Destiny Image Europe books are available at Christian bookstores and distributors worldwide.

To order products, or for any other correspondence:

DESTINY IMAGE® EUROPE
Via Acquacorrente, 6
65123 - Pescara - Italy
Tel. +39 085 4716623 - Fax: +39 085 4716622
E-mail: info@eurodestinyimage.com

Or reach us on the Internet:
www.eurodestinyimage.com

Dedication

To workplace ministers and their families.

Building a Marketplace Ministry

Poem by Kelsey R. Kerr
Age 13
December 25, 2002

Marketplace Ministers have it all down,
They know you don't have to be in church
to serve the guy with the crown.
The Bible says you can serve God from everywhere,
With God's eyes, He can see all ways you show you care.

When serving Him through the business world,
like He has anointed us to do,
There's more than just work involved, you show
others who lives in you.
God will bless you more and more, like
He has done with us,
All He wanted in return was our
complete surrendered trust.

He helps our families to understand and
helps them to stay strong,
It's a hard job, but they're great even when
everything seems wrong.
Our families stand beside us, as we
inch closer to success,
We know they are always there,
helping us to progress.

We thank our families for believing
and praying for us, too,

And more thanks goes to God for blessing
us through and through.

Building a Marketplace Ministry
is a great way to share,
Though it's just a business, we teach
people that God is there.

We work to fulfill God's desires,
just as He has planned,
Every step of the way, knowing we're
guided by His right hand.

We thank our Father for providing
during very tough times,
Such as the terrorist attack and
the impact of those crimes.

We pray that our children won't see us
as "money hungry" entrepreneurs,
But as servers of God's Kingdom because,
of course, that's what He prefers.

Written with a heart to glorify our God above,
We hope to encourage your great adventure, with love.
Some things happen for reasons we're unsure,
But with God, we know, they are always pure.

Table of Contents

Commendation

Acknowledgements

Foreword by Dr. Bill Hamon

Commendation

Is your occupation a never-ending drudgery? Or is it a divine assignment that enables you to move into your true destiny? Richard Fleming thinks that your work can be glorious, and he argues the point very convincingly in *The Glory Returns to the Workplace*. You will not go wrong by using this book as a road map to help you walk successfully through your life experience.

C. Peter Wagner, Presiding Apostle
International Coalition of Apostles

Acknowledgements

My thanks go to Mary De Bats, prophetic writer, for helping me write this book.

And further thanks to Charity Alberts for her final editing effort.

Love and thanks to my wife Pauline for creating the environment for writing, and not least for taking care of our workplace ministry on a day to day basis.

Blessings,
Richard

Foreword

Richard Fleming has done an outstanding job in presenting the truth of God's glory returning to the workplace. During the last two decades of the 20th-century Church, the Holy Spirit began to reveal God's desire and intent to restore His manifest presence in the workplace through Christians. The traditional theological concept of the church was that ministers in the pulpit had a calling to minister for Christ Jesus and see the Holy Spirit manifest within the four walls of the local church. This same traditionalism suggested that Christians in the secular workplace were not functioning in place of "ministry" and that the Holy Spirit did not manifest in the workplace like He did inside the four walls of the local church. Nevertheless the Holy Spirit has launched the 21st-century Church-through revelation and activation-into the purpose of the Church in the marketplace, in the public square of government, and the everyday workplace of the saints.

Now leaders are recognizing that the Church is wherever saints are functioning. There is only one Church of Jesus Christ on planet earth, but its sphere of influence can be described in these two categories: the "nuclear Church" and the "extended Church." The "nuclear Church" is the local Church which meets and functions inside the four walls of a building. However, the local Church is not defined by a physical building but by the saints who worship there. Saints functioning in the workplace are what we call the "extended Church" of Jesus Christ. Christians are Church members 24 hours a day, seven days a week. This means that Christians are functioning as the Church wherever they are and whatever they are doing in honest and upright work.

I have been propagating this truth for the past two decades and have supported it with biblical truth and experiential reality. Jesus is the same yesterday, today, and forever. He will manifest His glory in the workplace the same as He does within the local Church. Likewise, all of the gifts and graces of God are just as available to saints in the workplace as they are to saints in the pew of the local church. Jesus told us to pray and participate with God in making His will to be done on earth as it is being done in Heaven. For God's decree to be fulfilled-that the "glory of the Lord would fill the earth as the waters cover the sea"—then His glory must fill the "extended Church" the same as it does the "nuclear Church."

In this book you will not find a lot of theory and philosophy but living experiences of how the Holy Spirit manifests through saints that He might be glorified in the workplace. Read this book with an open heart and teachable mind for the truths found within it are revolutionary vis-a-vis traditional religious thinking. Richard reveals how the Holy Spirit has time and again prophetically expressed the heart and mind of God in these matters. I believe this book will be instrumental in enlightening and challenging the true Christian to cause God's glory to be returned to the workplace and thereby fill all of the earth with His glory. May all those who read this book receive the revelation and empowerment to restore God's glory in their places of work.

Dr. Bill Hamon
Chairman and Founder, *Christian International Ministries Network*
President, *Christian International Business Network*

CHAPTER 1

Enfranchising His Church in the Workplace

"We are in the throes of beginning to birth one of the most wrenching transitions that the Body of Christ has ever gone through."

—*Arthur Burk*

God is passionately interested in the marketplace. He is moving His people out into the workplace, across the whole community, and He is building His Church in these places. He is raising up workplace apostles, prophets, pastors, teachers and evangelists. These remarkable men and women of God are building the Church out in the world across every element of society. They are claiming the hospitals, businesses, areas of commerce, law enforcement, offices of trade, local and central government, science and technology, education and the court system back from Babylon for the Lord.

Church is not a building, a denomination or a series of services. The Church is the Body of Christ; those who march behind Him as their head. Church is comprised of the people of God working with

Him to bring His rule upon the earth. Where any two or three of the people of God are gathered, there Christ will be in the middle of them. There the Holy Spirit will flow, worship will be released, prayer will be offered, and a lifestyle of obedience will be demonstrated. The legitimate right to administrate communion and the covenant of marriage may exist wherever God's people are.

I work with God's apostles and leaders who are spearheading this reformation, who are working with God to take back every element of the cities and towns in which we live and work. I come alongside God's visionaries to help them realize their God-given destiny and find the fulfillment of His call upon them in the workplace.

This book is to encourage you that you have a destiny in God. That destiny can be outside the local church structure, and that there are people whom God is calling to help you to fulfill that purpose. It is also to tell the stories of a few people I am working with who are running hand-in-hand with God's purposes. I want you to know that you are not alone and that God is doing awesome things in this hour to prepare His people for what is to come in the days ahead.

Workplace Call

It was a conference for Christians in the workplace. Doctors, teachers, policemen, businessmen, entrepreneurs, homemakers—the whole range of different professions were represented among the thousands there. We were packed to capacity and many had been turned away. There was such a hunger and expectancy for God that throbbed through that place. I knew as I spoke that many were hurting and their callings were misunderstood.

I was prompted to say, "I know there are people in this hall today who are carrying a vision from God for their place of work in their heart, but it has been minimized and misunderstood, or others have tried to mold it into something they could understand or control. So much so that the light has nearly gone out. If that's you, please stand up now because the Holy Spirit wants to come and minister healing to you before we go any further." Over half the people stood up.

It is intensely personal and challenging to have the call of God upon you and have His vision planted in you by the Holy Spirit. But if the vision is then devalued, it causes deep wounds that only God can heal.

Wherever I go—America, Africa, Europe or the UK—I am encountering the same thing. God is instilling vision for so many people for their place of work, so we need to adjust our worldview in order to accommodate His challenges. As we present our vision to those with acknowledged Christian wisdom for advice and validation, all too often our vision is not recognized. The people we submit it to do not have the experience or the insight into our field of expertise to grasp its potential Kingdom impact.

Over months and years, the vision fades and closes down in us. As we struggle to serve God in ways that our peers understand, we settle for only a portion of our destiny and relegate the unlived dreams we had to the dustbin of painful memories. In these days God is asking us to adjust our binoculars and refocus our hearts upon His strategies for the world He loves so deeply. So often we wrongly assume we know His strategies, or that nothing will change. But, our God is a God of new wineskins and He is always moving forward to reach out to us, and those about us in new and different ways.

This book is a prophetic encounter with the future that we can build in our world if we choose. The future is a road that, if we choose to walk down it, opens a door to the release of Kingdom life and new hope into the world in which we live and work. It is not necessarily an easy pathway, but it is one that leads to a life of destiny and purpose. It leads from the football pitch to the executive suite and from the classroom to the schools of revival.

This is the recipe for a Kingdom extravaganza—if we choose to accept God's challenge and run with Him. There are no guarantees it will work the way we expect, but we have His promised partnership that He will be with us, and that where He is, there is a true peace which we can find in none other.

Challenged by a Call to Work

I see many people who are struggling to grasp hold of what God has for them. People hear the call of God and assume it is a call to full-time church leadership. So often though it is a call to full-time workplace leadership. We have believed too long that the Church has one structure or model. One couple who grasped the diversity of the Church was Paul and Catherine. Paul is a senior information technology consultant for a multinational consulting company. When they heard this message, Paul said something in him just sparked. Catherine also knew this teaching held the key for them.

From an early age, Paul had felt called into the ministry, yet the place where he seemed to be having more and more success was work. They were trying to juggle their lives of being very involved in the local church, which they found satisfying, with also being very involved at work and getting more so. They could not understand why there was this draw toward work and why the doors were opening there. All they had really ever thought they would do would be to go into full-time pulpit ministry together.

Paul and Catherine's Journey

Paul explains how God brought revelation to him and Catherine.

"We asked Richard to meet with us to go through what the Lord had been saying to us and what had been happening in our lives. That evening he did what nobody had ever done for us. He sat and listened to all our prophetic words and made notes. He asked what had been happening at work. He just drew out of me all the capabilities, and the doors that had been opening for me, and wrote a list of all the key things that I had been demonstrating time after time at work.

"As we listened to our prophetic words and dreams, we realized the direction was not for 'local church ministry,' but through my full-time ministry in the workplace. I had words about being apostolic and a lot of what I was doing at work was pioneering, breaking ground, making a path for others to walk on. I was supplying an apostolic covering to people at work and to the business. Also God had called me to speak out of revelation. We've seen it happen again and again. We thought it had to be in a local church context, but often at work I'm just speaking revelation, even into people's lives.

"One area of responsibility at work is career management. I have that responsibility over my business unit because I have an ability to pastor people. In the local church we lead a cell group. We were part of the leadership team and I was involved in leading one of the plant out congregations. So you could look at what we were doing in the local church and say we were well on the way to achieving that vision of being in ministry. Yet there was still something that wasn't there. It was as if the more we did, the more we were not satisfied. People would say, 'you'll lead a church,' and we would say, 'we don't want to lead a church.' It was really odd. We knew the local church pathway wasn't right for us.

"There was just a sense of confusion, especially since I came from a family of church leaders whose ministry was out in the community. In my family roots there are medical people, doctors, etc., who became missionaries and went to places other people hadn't heard of. For example, my grandfather had pioneered as a surgeon in China where they had never heard the gospel. My uncle went to Bangladesh as a mission doctor and still works as a doctor in the Bangladeshi community in the East End of London.

"So as I looked back into my family I began to see that my ministry heritage wasn't just confined to being a churchman. Richard opened up the understanding that ministry is about your whole life. We'd just fallen into the mindset of seeing ministry only in the context of the local church. Now it seems so ridiculous that we could possibly have thought that, but since our view has been enlarged we've found others who are in the same situation and have this limited view of what ministry is about. They don't sit comfortably in a local church, as they feel guilty all the time because they feel motivated to be at work. They say, 'we feel like we don't fit.' It's absolutely amazing. So many people still don't have the understanding that we are the Church wherever we are.

"That revelation has changed our lives. It seemed to be so absolutely radical. As part of walking out this revelation, Catherine and I knew we were to minister shoulder to shoulder. Catherine's main area was prayer, making a highway in the heavenlies. We began realizing that we already did that quite naturally in the workplace. Once when I was on site and the computers were in danger of being thrown off site, I just laid hands on them and prayed and rang Catherine and she prayed. Within hours the whole situation was turned around and the computers stayed and we were given more work.

"We've found again and again that when we would pray about situations at work and take authority, the doors would open or whatever needed to happen would happen. It opened up a very different viewpoint for us. No longer was work something that I went to just to pay the bills for us to do whatever in the local church. That was a big change.

"I felt challenged as to how much involvement I could have with people either at work or at my local church. Obviously at work you're with people 40-odd hours a week and you get into some fairly intense situations and relationships really form. Also, there are other people I am in contact with, such as clients and suppliers. We realized in the local church, by comparison, even with really committed people we would only get up to ten hours a week to put into these people and pastor them. You get so much more time at work and in less formal situation.

"Another aspect was, where was I most able to operate in my prophetic and pastoral giftings? So often you're just in the right place at the right time for people at work. You can't be as easily in a church service situation. During the September 11th terrorist attacks, I spent the whole afternoon pastoring people—it was incredible. One of the key men I was working with in the States was stuck in Seattle. I spent ages on the phone to him, as he was so shocked. He and his wife couldn't get hold of good friends in New York and didn't know what was happening to them. He was on the other side of the States from his wife and she just needed her husband. He was saying on the phone, 'Paul if you keep talking to me like this, I'm gonna cry.' It's not what someone typically says at work. But when these types of things happen you realize this is what it's all about. We have found those opportunities at work in a most extraordinary way.

"We realized we had confined church to a Sunday, a particular building and set of people, but so often I ended up having church in my own office with people who didn't even know the Lord. All those opportunities are there for me to call people together and see the Kingdom of God break out.

"At a workplace conference Catherine and I attended, pastors were repenting for portraying the idea that 'you can go off to work to finance the local church, but the really important thing is what you're doing in the local church. Come and do our vision and do our activity and everything will be fine.' I sat there watching and suddenly felt the Lord bring conviction to my heart that actually it wasn't just the pastors who thought that—I thought that also. That view is held just as much by the people as the pastors. Yes, there needs to be revelation for local church leaders, but there also needs to be revelation for me.

Another idea we're just beginning to grapple with is that the field the Lord has called us to is actually a secular company rather than starting our own business. There is a different set of challenges in a completely secular context. God has called me to the workplace and that can take as many hours and as much responsibility as running our own company, or even more since I don't have my own prayer room at work and can't stop business to battle stuff through. I have to come home and battle for the business in order to demonstrate that the power of God is effective and to have people challenged and changed by that.

"As we took this new mindset on board and started to walk it out, things began to happen. I realized if I was physically on site with the client, things went much more smoothly than if I was called away. Often if I was in a different office for a day something major would go pear-shaped. Catherine and I started to bind the principalities and powers at work in that company and take authority from a distance rather than our presence on site. There was definitely an authority flowing that I didn't even realize.

"There was one particularly difficult project situation that arose. I came face-to-face with this intense spiritual battle. I have to be honest; it almost wrecked me. I have never felt so stressed in all my life. You realize that doing battle out in the secular world, there's the potential to be a casualty yourself, even though you're plugged into the Lord. As the project went on, the company we were doing the project for ran into financial difficulties. By this stage it was a very high-pressure job. Catherine felt God speak to her about Peter in prison and how God opened the doors miraculously, but Peter didn't just run out, he collected his things. He put on his cloak and sandals. He put on what belonged to him and then he walked out of prison.

"She began to pray that into the situation. The difficulty of the project with the physical and spiritual oppression made it feel like being in prison. The company wasn't paying their bills, so she started to pray that the prison doors would be open and I would gather what was owed to me. It took a while but the company paid their bills and it ended up being a very profitable project. One of the things I had been passionate about was that this project would be successful from a financial perspective for my company. During that period we certainly watched the grace of God in operation, as He delivered what I could not.

"Richard spoke about hearing God in the marketplace and the business network, but it was God who put it in us—we just knew. Up until then the subject of work didn't have much relevance to a church context. It was a necessary evil that took us away from other things that we could be doing for 40 hours a week. Then God woke us up and suddenly it was something completely different. It was bringing a sense of life and purpose and call to what I was spending the bulk of my life doing. Instead of wading through the week with a sense of frustration and guilt, I felt a release of ministry at work which brought life and freedom."

What's God up to in Your Workplace?

Paul and Catherine have demonstrated God's power in their workplace, but God's grace is there for everyone. Whether you are one of God's visionaries, or you are walking out your gifts and calling at work, all Christians can and should expect to see God's hand in all we do. I want to challenge you: how actively involved do you think God is in your work life right now? How much do you talk to Him about what's happening there? How much do you listen to His answers to your questions?

The first time God broke into my work life I almost rejected what He did, expecting I was being duped rather than immediately recognizing the Lord's direction at work. I was in the process of selling and leasing back our car fleet and one morning God spoke to me and said,

"Let Me show you how I can make a profit for you. Go into work as usual, but all you are to do is to read your Bible."

So I went into work daily as usual and read my Bible. I did nothing else. My personal assistant at that time was my wife, Pauline, and she was not at all happy with my behavior. "You call yourself a Christian?" she said. I just kept my head down and continued doing what I knew God had asked me to do. We had four proposals out for the selling and leaseback of our car fleet and three offers had come in. Each offer was giving us around £80,000 cashback and they were all broadly the same for the monthly leaseback costs.

Then, at the end of my week of Bible reading, we got the fourth proposal in. This one gave us £180,000 cashback for the same rental. So the rentals were equal but there was this £100,000 difference. I, and my financial director, who was also a Christian, poured over this contract for two weeks, not wanting to accept it because we thought it was a con. In the end we had to come to the conclusion that God had worked a miracle. The company had 250 staff and made annual profits of £500,000. In one week, God produced one-fifth of our annual profit in response to me being obedient to what He said. God had my attention and it started me on a journey. I told Him, "God, you're proving to me that you're in my work and I want to cooperate with You in this." Since then I've had miracle after miracle after miracle.

So many people today think God limits His involvement in the world's marketplace to people's relationships and integrity. He is deeply interested in both those aspects of course, but in my experience our God is interested in all our work activities. He wants to make us prosper. He is calling for His people to go into their workplaces and bring His life there. It is about possessing and governing our territory His way. We all know the scriptural mandate, and while few of us apply it to our workplaces, the Bible is clear in Genesis 1:28—we were not only created to work but also to possess our places of work.

He Who Calls Is Able

God is calling us into that place in the Spirit where the Lord pours out vision, hope and passion into His people and where He stands guard over His visionaries, providing for them in supernatural ways and raising them up to spearhead His revival in the cities where we live.

No one has said working with God will be easy—in human terms faith frequently wobbles when challenges come—and let's not pretend the mighty hand of the Lord won't test and refine us along the way. Let's acknowledge that He who calls is able and willing to keep safe the one upon whom He places His calling and that He who envisions is able and is willing to provide all that is needed to fulfill the vision He gives. Money, contacts, open doors and people—He alone is the provider of it all.

I worked at the Christian television station called the God Channel for a while and there were times during my season when we simply would not have been able to continue had it not been for God's hand of timely intervention providing us with money and contacts or whatever we needed. It was a tough time, but the Lord moved repeatedly to support the vision He had given. The God Channel at that time was still in its infancy and the books weren't even balanced yet, but God repeatedly broke in and kept us afloat.

We worked out of the Family Channel studios in Kent and I was traveling there each week from Birmingham. The distance was almost enough to keep me from going. Money was very tight, but we were managing to service our creditors. Then the ownership of the Family Channel studios was taken over by another company, one of the main media companies today, and a load of new people came in. They saw at once that we were there on a dream ticket. Nevertheless for the first five months God enabled me to negotiate a no-cost for our edit suite. When these new owners came in they really wanted us out. So much so that they chose to break the news when we were in the middle of preparing for the dedication of the God Channel and were planning to have 3,000 people come from across Europe for it. The new people told us that unless we paid the great sum we owed them in ten days, they were going to pull the plug on our telephone system.

We pointed out that we were about to do this big event and that we had people ringing in from all over Europe, but of course they did not see that as their problem. Well, that could have been the end for us, but God intervened and did some reprogramming to help us. We got a call from Morris Cerullo in America and he asked to be moved out of his hour's prime slot on Sunday morning into two vacant half-hour slots. God moved TBN into that hour slot and helped me negotiate an up-front payment three times larger than we owed, which went on the owner's desks within the ten days. We were able to celebrate our dedication as planned.

God intervened again when we needed a charity number in about a week. We got a phone call from our media consultant saying he knew a man who operated a charity to raise money for Christian television. I asked, "why don't they talk to us, we're the first Christian channel in the U.K?" The bottom line was that they transferred to us their charity with a positive balance in the bank and we were able to put their charity number on our literature.

It all happened because a number of years earlier God raised up three retired civil servants to set up and register the first Christian television (CTV) charity, called Angel Christian Television Trust. They blessed us with their work and vision as they gave the charity to us.

We had miracle after miracle, which began to increase my understanding that God is interested in every element of the workplace and that He will anoint people to do whatever He needs to get done. He will achieve His purpose.

Transforming Territories

When we look at the scriptural mandate found in Genesis 1:28, *"fill the earth and subdue the land,"* and translate this through the fall of man and the resurrection power of Jesus Christ, we are called to fill the earth with people of God's Spirit. It is what we are called to do in our workplaces, just as we are called to do in every area of our lives. We are called to change territories and fill our workplaces with people of God's Spirit.

Tell It Again

I wanted to include a story I first heard from my friend Rich Marshall that I hope will change our mindsets and challenge the box we have put God inside.

This is the story of how one businessman in the Philippines has dramatically changed his God-given territory since he became a Christian. Like so many stories, it all begins with prayer. One lady took it upon herself to pray for this man's salvation. God heard and acted and one day she was able to lead him to the Lord. However, he had a dubious means of support. His company owned 20 motels and one hotel. In the Philippines at that time, motel rooms were rented with a roommate. So effectively, 20 of his 21 units were places of prostitution. This man had 2,000 staff in total, and most of them were in prostitution as the only means of supporting their families.

A. Having led the man to the Lord and knowing how many local church people would not be able to accept his occupation and thus tell him to retire all the prostitutes, the lady instead discipled him herself and he sought God for how he could turn his business into a righteous enterprise.

B. The Lord's strategy was that the businessman transforms each motel/brothel one by one, leading the employees to the Lord. Seven years later, 19 of the 20 motels are now transformed. Seventeen hundred of his 2,000 staff members are born again and he has a full-time pastor in charge of each motel unit, leading church in the workplace. All the staff members have kept their income stream flowing, maintaining support for their families; they are no longer in prostitution, for the businessman has retrained them into other jobs. He has helped them to be healed by the hand of the Lord, and he has sought to bind up their brokenness.

C. Few of us would even think of taking biblical principles to such extremes. Most people today would have just gotten rid of the prostitutes, yet through doing what God asked him to do he has seen miracles of transformation among his people and he is now prospering mightily. Rich Marshall asked him to come to America to give his testimony, but he has refused, saying that he felt the Lord was telling him not to give personal testimony until all 2,000 of his people were born again. His intercessors confirmed what he felt he was hearing, so he has held back from speaking personally, although he did give Rich Marshall permission to tell the story.

D. He has also devised a pastor's training program for his pastors, to enable them to cope with the peculiar nature of the brokenness and problems of his people—pimps, drugs, dysfunctional relationships, childhood abuse, etc. This training program is regarded in the area as the leading teaching program for pastors.

E. What better example could you have of the fulfillment of the mandate to go and fill the earth? The transformation, habitation and harvesting of souls at such a business fills the land with people of the same Spirit. That scriptural mandate is in full operation in a formerly corrupt and depraved area of the earth. No wonder the businessman has faith for 100% of his staff to get saved.

Who Are You?

What about you? My guess is that some people reading this book have a calling from God in their heart to make a difference in their workplace, city or nation. But perhaps you're wrestling with the credibility gap that says your dream doesn't sit well with what you have experienced in local church or that it's not spiritual enough to be from God.

Maybe you are searching in the dark to find and fulfill your God-given identity, but at this moment you are feeling stuck and getting more exasperated with a system that doesn't seem to work for you. Perhaps you are struggling to bring God's heart and power to your working environment, but have never felt commissioned, ordained, trained, or supported in your vision by the local Christian community.

Are you are a local church leader who has become frustrated that in spite of all your church's efforts, nothing has significantly shifted in your town or region? Do you see current city-reaching strategies failing to sustain substantive impact? If that's you, then be encouraged because God is on the move.

God is changing mindsets, opening doors of opportunity and moving in power to undertake for those He is releasing to minister in the workplace. And through this initiative He is moving to change even the hearts of nations in this hour. It is too narrow a vision for God's workplace visionaries to limit themselves to righteous government of their company and to making money. God is dealing in these days in terms of city- and territory-taking.

He is envisioning people with new ways of instituting government for their workplaces. He is birthing new inventions and new products in people's hearts. He is putting new hearts in us, soft hearts for the people of the territories we occupy. As we pray, God burdens our hearts for those within our territories, and we reach out into the city streets around us.

Groups of people from different expressions of calling, including business, health, commerce, social work and government, are working together to heal the broken heart of the city. God is calling us to be His body, His hands, His heart and His church in the city.

We have tried to segregate the spiritual from the rest of life, particularly our working life. We have been content simply to aim for righteousness rather than allowing the Spirit who dwells within us to unleash His power through us to affect the very atmosphere we breathe. When we live out our working lives in the power of the Spirit we find ourselves empowered to fulfill a God-given vision, speaking prophetically into commercial situations and the lives of those about us.

We find ourselves in prayer, tearing down strongholds that stand against our success. We rise up in His authority to lay claim to, and grasp hold of, the financial resources He pours out to fulfill the vision. This is living out the life of Kingdom business day by day as we tread the ground of our destiny, possessing the land and occupying every place we put our feet. That's what it's all about. That's what God is releasing into the land at this present time, this new church season of taking possession of the land and occupying it for His purpose. It is church building as He designed it.

Josiahs and Joshuas: Who, Me?

God's plan has always been to change the heart of territories and to bring in His Kingdom rule. Much of the Old Testament is the story of the people of God falling away from Him and relaxing their efforts to bring His life to their land, then God in response lifting His hand from them so they found themselves falling prey to all kinds of oppression. Then they turned once more to the Lord and He forgave them and poured out blessing on them.

One story that always gets my attention is that of Josiah, who changed his nation and turned them back to God when he was only 18 years old. Although the change was only during his lifetime and the judgement averted only until the nation turned away again, God heard and responded to Josiah's willing and humble heart. If God could change a nation with one 18-year-old then He can just as surely do it again today.

Josiah learned the heart of God through studying the written word, the Law given to Moses. He then sought guidance from God through His spoken word and thirdly he humbly obeyed all he understood God to be asking of him. The result was peace for the nation and the favor of God upon them. For today's workplace kings the requirements are the same: to seek the Scriptures for God's heart, to seek God for personal vision and specific guidance. Once these are grasped hold of by faith, we need to be humbly obedient to all He is asking of us.

In the calling of God we are all at different stages on the road to fulfillment, but God has set before each one of us a promised land here on earth, a territory set aside for us to conquer and subdue and fill with people of like Spirit.

In Deuteronomy 11:10-12, God tells us about our Promised Land, the territory we are to occupy for Him:

> *For the land which you go in to possess is not like the land of Egypt, from which you came out, where you sowed your seed and watered it with your foot laboriously as in a garden of vegetables. But the land which you enter to possess is a land of hills and valleys which drinks water of the rain of the heavens, A land for which the Lord your God cares; the eyes*

of the Lord your God are always upon it from the beginning
of the year to the end of the year.

For most of us the land into which we will go and find the hand of
God tending and watering is our workplace. That's where we spend
most of our waking hours. That's where we earn our living. That's
where the ungodly tribes and wild beasts are. This is where we will
find ourselves walking in the power of God to fulfill the scriptural
mandate for our personal lives.

Our promised land will be a physical place, but the context is
spiritual. We go into our promised workplace land, knowing that to
possess and inhabit the land we have to drive out the wild beasts and the
existing idolatry. This is a spiritual reference to satan's occupancy by
false mindsets and ungodly thinking, not actual people and their jobs.

All of us are on a journey from our Egypt, through the desert
regions into our Promised Land. Egypt was the place we were in and
we were used to. The desert is our training ground, the place we learn
to follow God, hear His voice and trust His leading for us. Once we've
crossed the Jordan, we enter our Promised Land and there we find a
Joshua anointing in our hands to help us take, occupy and govern this
place of our fulfillment.

The promises God makes to us about His provision for us in our
place of fulfillment are overwhelming. Deuteronomy 11:13-15 says,

> *And if you will diligently heed My commandments which I*
> *command you this day, to love the Lord your God and to*
> *serve Him with all your [mind and] heart and with your*
> *entire being, I will give the rain for your land in its season,*
> *the early rain and the latter rain, that you may gather in your*
> *grain, your new wine, and your oil. And I will give grass in*
> *your fields for your cattle, that you may eat and be full.*

Later in the chapter God adds to His promises. In Deuteronomy
11:22-27, God promises:

> *For if you diligently keep all this commandment which I com-*
> *mand you to do, to love the Lord your God, to walk in all His*
> *ways, and to cleave to Him.*

Then the Lord will drive out all these nations before you, and you shall dispossess nations greater and mightier than you. Every place upon which the sole of your foot shall tread shall be yours: from the wilderness to Lebanon, and from the River, the river Euphrates, to the western sea [the Mediterranean] your territory shall be. There shall no man be able to stand before you; the Lord your God shall lay the fear and the dread of you upon all the land that you shall tread, as He has said to you. Behold, I set before you this day a blessing and a curse. The blessing if you obey the commandments of the Lord your God which I command you this day...

There are also the warnings against turning away from God and being disobedient to His word to us (see Deut. 11:16-17,28).

Do you hear what He's saying to you? It's exciting once it gets inside you. God is taking each one of you to a promised land, pre-ordained and set aside by His hand for you to occupy. Once you get there He is going to be with you in every way. God's eye is on the place closely watching over it. He is making Himself personally responsible for the provision of all the resources you need. He is promising bountiful harvest, He promises prosperity and He offers you great territory. He Himself undertakes to help you overcome all opposition to the establishing of His Kingdom rule as you occupy the land. His promises are clear, but we need to grasp hold of them and work with Him.

Like Joshua we need to know and understand how to work with God to take the territory He has given us in order to occupy and rule the land. Like Joshua we need to keep a close relationship with the Lord, to know and trust His voice and to be humbly obedient to all He asks us to do. Once we enter our promised land we need to know in our hearts that the Lord is present and letting us work alongside Him to accomplish His purpose in our given territory.

Just as God provided for us when I was with the God Channel, just as the Lord enabled the motel owner in the Philippines to change his promised land and drive out the former inhabitants, just as He gave me one-fifth of my annual profits in one week of Bible reading obedience, so each one of us has God's promise of power in us to fulfill our destiny for Him.

Maybe you've never thought of yourself as a workplace warrior, a Joshua to take territory from the enemy and to inhabit and subdue the land. You probably never thought of your workplace as a nation that God has called you as king to change as Josiah did. We don't think of ourselves in that way, but God does. He knows who He made you to be. He knows the plans and the destiny He made you for. As Jeremiah 29:11 prophecies,

> *I alone know My purpose for you, says the Lord: prosperity and not misfortune, and a long line of children after you.*

Don't just take my word for it; talk to the people who are out there doing it. One thing is certain: when you follow the call of God in the workplace, He is with you and things start to happen.

Go to Work; Go to Church

Of course, talking about possessing and occupying is easy, but doing it is another matter. Throughout the centuries the Church has mostly failed to significantly impact the workplace environment. There have been individuals who have extremely impacted specific social working conditions. They have abolished slavery and they have brought about child labor reforms. Today, rather than just social reform, we desire to impact the whole of the workplace with the life of Christ.

The Quakers have had some great impact on specific companies when they were run by Quaker businessmen on biblical principles. But even taken together, the impact of these faithful men and women of God has not touched the life of cities as a whole. The Church has physically conquered through war, invasions and crusades, but for the most part this brought a domination by physical force and persecution that centuries later, we are trying to repair spiritually through repentance and reconciliation. God doesn't want to violate our own free will—He is looking for those who will freely choose Him.

The Church has a great impact in an area by being a relationally based church in the community. But where are the relationally based churches in the workplace communities of our cities today? Well, they are small and few, but they are starting to appear as God moves to build His Church—a church that will defeat the counterfeit kingdom rule of the workplace with His power. Gradually we are seeing God raise up workplace ministers, evangelists, pastors, teachers, apostles and prophets.

I believe **1**: apostles and prophets called to the church in the workplace, and **2**: being an integral part of the one citywide church made up of many fellowships and congregations, is as big a paradigm shift for the established Church of today as when Peter was released to take salvation to the Gentiles.

Peter Wagner, in his book *Apostles and Prophets*, identified marketplace apostles as the fourth category of apostles; vertical apostles, horizontal apostles and hyphenated apostles being the other three. We are on the radar and more and more activity is being detected and discussed.

Peter Wagner goes on to say: "I will be surprised if the ministry of marketplace apostles does not become one of the hot topics over the next few years. I believe in it so strongly that I have been bold enough to include marketplace ministries as one of the elective concentrations in my new school, Wagner Leadership Institute."

He also says, "I believe there are apostles of finance, technology, medicine, industry, education, the military, government, law, communications, business, transportation, nuclear science, agriculture and a hundred other segments of society. When these marketplace apostles begin to move into their rightful place under the powerful anointing of God, watch out! Revival will be right around the corner." [1]

I am excited to see the way God is raising up new types of churches as we move into the end times, but I also want to keep anchoring that in the hands-on experience of how we are seeing God move at this time. I am currently working with three different types of churches that God is blessing in the workplace, whose main focus is to bring the life of Christ to the marketplace communities of our towns and cities.

For want of better descriptive terms, we refer to these churches as workplace churches, Kingdom advice centers and incubator churches.

These churches aim to express Christ throughout every structure and organization within the city.

Workplace Churches

The workplace church is a structural organization with a place and function in the city. Although it has a temple-based heart, it also expends much energy on habitation and harvest activities; it is city-focused. It works the land for the benefit of the city and interacts with the city on the natural as well as the supernatural level. The people that corporate churches reach are on their plot of land and they come into touch with them naturally through business and workplace networking relationships.

There are always supernatural relationships. The workplace church happens at work during working hours or lunch breaks, focused around the gathering of wealth and building an influence base.

> "The workplace church is legitimized by the Word of God, by encompassing gatherings, five-fold ordained leadership, mercy missions and evangelism. It would be a confining point of view to consider the marketplace church as a business persons' meeting or a para-church organization. It is one of the new apostolic shapes of church today. Unfortunately, a new wineskin often brings territorial challenges before regional cooperation. There will be those that doubt the legitimacy of the workplace church because some will leave their existing congregations. It will look like separation before it looks like multiplication. The workplace church is necessary for this time. Because of it's passion for wealth transfer and kingdom projects, it will radically transform our cities into a demonstration of God and Kingdom lifestyle."
>
> *Dr. Sharon Stone*

Kingdom Advice Centers

These centers of excellence are for apostolic and prophetic input. They are teaching resources to train the trainers of tomorrow. They do not have a local congregation, but are set up as a training and advice resource for apostolic and prophetic input to help individuals and company groups grasp hold of God's vision for them. Clients come for different reasons. Workplace and local church leaders can come for training in workplace skills here. People attend for different lengths of time depending on how long it takes them to become mature in ministering the gifts.

For example, it only takes students about a year to reach an intellectual understanding of hearing the voice of God, but it takes about two years for people to grow and become confident in the prophetic. Kingdom advice centers are relationally based rather than territory based and will send a fivefold ministry team to a client's place of work to help them build.

Team members support and stand alongside the workplace or marketplace visionary, looking to bring their corporate power to his authority, and to bring the collective anointing of the Kingdom advice center to his workplace. It should bring an addition to his field and establish the foundation of church in that place. The collective knowledge and understanding within the Kingdom advice center should be transferred.

Incubator Churches

The incubator church is a local church that has trained its leaders to help equip and maximize the God-given potential of each of the people who make up their congregation. They disciple people to find and fulfill their God-given vision, eventually releasing them to start church in their own workplace. They then make their own disciples, nurturing them through learning to hear the voice of God, understanding their destiny, finding their field and stepping out into the fullness of their vision.

Basically, the incubator church is a training, equipping and releasing church whose purpose is to release leaders of the Body of Christ into the fullness of their individual callings in **the workplace rather than the pulpit.** The incubator church is a birthing and launching center for workplace ministers.

People enter the Incubator Church school of the prophets to learn to hear God's voice where they work from day one after being converted.

They are helped to take the calling they hear from God and place it in the context of destiny. They are shown how to find their field and marry their call to the land. Some incubator churches and Kingdom advice centers also help by providing starter pots, or incubator units where people can get established in a fairly closeted environment before being launched into the world.

God Is Changing Church

God is changing the face of His Church. The cry for change is rising up from across the globe. No one is certain of what or how many new shapes there will be, but even at this stage of its evolution some things are becoming clear. The world over, the Lord's visionaries are seeking to discern the new shape of church for the age that we are now entering. No one man has the whole vision, but we hear the same cries rising up across the globe.

The vision has to do with territory, with cities and the taking of whole areas at once for the Kingdom of God. It has to do with the outpouring of the Spirit in these last days, calling the people of God into sustained prayer and worship and calling for His coming. It has to do with the passion in the heart of God for those who do not yet know Him. And it has to do with the fulfillment of the redemptive purposes of cities and nations in these last days.

It is about the Body of Christ rising up to touch the heart of every organization, structure and people group within cities and nations. It has to do with the sovereignty of God expressed in an expansive outpouring of His abundant love toward His image bearers who populate His earth, His work in creation.

Certainly it is clear that the shape and form of the Church today is not the complete shape and form of the Church that will enforce dominion over all the kingdoms of this world. My heart is for the workplace and I see these new marketplace churches having a major role in accomplishing this aim, for they take dominion in education, technology and sciences, industry and commerce, health, law and order, media, business and government.

These are the dominions, made up of spheres of operation that the Word of God talks about in 1 Corinthians 12:6-7:

There are different distributions of divine energy, motivating these gifts and in their operation, but the same God who by his divine energy operates them all in their sphere, but to each one there is constantly being given the clearly seen operations of the spirit with a view to the profit of all.

These are the spheres of operation that cumulatively make up the dominion of this world; ones that our Bible says have been given to the saints of the most High God.

I have a dream from God to see fivefold marketplace ministers training and discipling the church in the marketplace, and the saints enforcing victory and taking territory in concrete kingdoms like their workplace or conceptual kingdoms like the media. Workplace churches can be resourced by Kingdom advice centers and incubator churches, which will function as apostolic and prophetic centers that are open day and night to provide fivefold ministry support in the marketplace.

We do not know the final shape or form, but Revelation 21:22 gives us some clues as to where we are going: *"But I saw no temple in it for the Lord God Almighty and the Lamb are its temple."* So we are about to set out on an adventure that will begin to fulfill the process and structure of the last days Church, that risen church built on the foundations of apostles and prophets, releasing the saints movement and the army of God, supported by the marketplace fivefold ministry, to enforce Christ's dominion in every area.

The world needs what this type of church can do. This kind of church demonstrates Christ in every element of a city. This church has the competence under the lordship of Christ to run a city and nation. This kind of church can enter any education establishment, any health authority, any business, any government, any media empire, and under the lordship of Christ, give the right answer. This kind of church is one the world will come to for answers. This world will queue outside the doors of the church that can give them the answers.

I prophesy to you that Jesus is leading His Church through a paradigm shift to a shape and form that will enfranchise the marketplace. He is loosing His marketplace apostles and prophets to build His

Church alongside His pulpit apostles and prophets. It is here that we will find the people who will go and *"be fruitful and multiply, and fill the earth, and subdue it; and rule over the fish of the sea and over the birds of the sky and over every living thing that moves on the earth,"* according to Genesis 1:28.

The people of the marketplace church have been strategically positioned for the end times. They have the buildings, they have the money, they have the influence and interaction with the world at every level of society, and just as importantly they are paid to spend an average of 50 hours every week there.

Endnote

1. Peter Wagner, *Apostles and Prophets* (Ventura, CA: Gospel Light Pubns, 2000)

CHAPTER 2

Your Personal Promised Land

Are you called to be God's steward of His workplace purposes? Do you carry a vision from God for a territory, company or workplace sector? God's purposes for these days are awesome. Prophets, Bible readers and Christian thinkers across the world are all proclaiming the same message—the end times are upon us and we must prepare for God to do the mighty deeds He has promised. We are about to engage in spiritual warfare like we have never previously understood. Get ready, for the Lord's purposes are coming to pass, ready or not.

It seems that the workplace is one of the places where God's refining comes right in your face, and often just when you think you most need His encouragement. Through it all God builds a new level of trust and dependence on Him. Relationship with Him is the key to fulfillment of vision in the workplace as it is in any other field of endeavor for the Lord.

Intimacy is the key to hearing, seeing and obeying. We learn to walk in His strength and trust in His person to take us through. It is common to all our stories. God works with His people today exactly as

He did in the Bible. Joshua, Gideon, Samson, Daniel, Jehoshaphat and others, are all stories we see reflected in the lives of today's generation.

Of course there are always challenges in finding our destiny, but there are also challenges in walking it out to bring the vision and God's purposes through to fulfillment. Whether your vision is for yourself as an individual, for your company, for your city or for your nation, the challenges will be there in proportion to the type of calling God has placed upon you.

Survivor or Warrior

The question is, who are you: survivor or warrior? Have you heard the Gideon call of God that draws you out of your existing lifestyle into the exciting challenges God has for you?

In Judges 6:11-40, Gideon is hiding from the Midianites to thresh his wheat. In verse 12 it says,

> *Then the Angel of the Lord appeared to him and said to him, "The Lord is with you, you mighty man of fearless courage."*

The last thing Gideon feels like is a mighty warrior. He's hiding in the winepress to thresh the wheat so the Midianites don't find it and take it.

He's living in a territory occupied by the enemy and he's feeling like he's at the back of beyond and going nowhere. He's a "nobody" in his own eyes and in the eyes of those around him. Are you relating to this? Most of us find that the workplace is in the camp of the enemy and we are trying to get the job done without provoking the enemy or hiding our Christian identity from people as to not get found out, laughed at and robbed. But God's greeting is unequivocal. '*The Lord is with you mighty man of fearless courage.*'

Gideon's spirit heard the greeting of God and responded by rising up within him. So it is with us today. When God speaks, He imparts something of His heart for us, something of His belief in us and our faith rises in response. God has no illusions about us. He knows the failures, the things we'd rather not be doing, the things we've left on one side, and the stuff we've shelved off onto others. He knows where we've cheated Him, and He still loves us.

He still sees us as His mighty warriors. He still calls to us to be the mighty warriors He made us to be. And from deep within our spirits we feel ourselves rising up to meet that challenge. Maybe it took us 20 years to hear His call, maybe we got it 20 seconds after being saved— it makes no difference. Once we've heard it, our spirits rise to meet His expectations of us. We push aside our own realities to walk into His.

Unfortunately the world is full of people who have heard the calling of God but have not been able to fulfill the dream He's planted within them. Often it is because the church leaders have not understood the calling as being from God since it came for a sector they perceived as unimportant. Maybe it has simply been a case of the visionary being unable to stir themselves up to leave their comfort zone, with their comfortable home and family life, and step out of their survival mentality to take up the sword of the warrior.

Sometimes people have taken it up too soon, rushing in hopefully, but not understanding God's timing and His wisdom for their lives, nor understanding His training and the hard paths He so often calls His warriors to walk.

Walking in the Challenge

Gideon's realignment of his self-image did not come overnight. His first assignment he carried out under cover of darkness for fear his own community would reject him. So often in the workplace today we find we have to push forward with God's vision on our own. It is the visionary who has to carry the vision and he has to be prepared to do it alone, though usually people come alongside when success bites!

Everyone loves a winner and so it was with Gideon. Once he started winning, the nation followed him. That first step out in obedience he had to stand against the village, but his father's wisdom saved him from being cut to pieces. In verse 31 Joash says,

If Baal be a god, let him contend for himself because one has pulled down his altar.

And by the grace of God's hand and the threat of death from the hand of Joash, the people agreed and Gideon was spared.

Today we also are dependent upon courage, wisdom and our Father to stand with us. The one thing that is certain is that there will be contention for any vision that comes directly from God. If God is calling you to install His vision in your workplace, you can be sure that someone, somewhere will contend with you for it. But from looking at Gideon's story we can see that he pushed forward in spite of all and won through, leading Israel to great victories and freedom from their enemies.

One man, who found out how hard the challenges can be at a personal level, is Edward of Ghana. Edward knew God wanted to bless him in business and at first all seemed to be going well. He had been given several prophetic words in the U.S. about how God wanted him to demolish old buildings, replace them with high-rises, and to clad them. Back in Ghana he started winning contracts for his building products and he knew the hand of God had to be with him or he would not have succeeded as he did. Business was booming. But then everything changed when God opened the door for him to bid for a very large contract, which he won. It was a turning point. Corrupt government officials suddenly started to take notice of him. Twelve million dollars worth of contracts stirred up their interest big-time.

God's Hand in the Desert

Edward was contracted to supply and hang glass curtain walling on several new tower blocks. All was going well until one day he had an unpleasant visit. The visitors turned out to be government officials, who had tried to cut him out of the business by dealing direct with the original suppliers of the product. When the American suppliers refused to renege on their deal with Edward, the officials tried other ways of taking Edward's lucrative business.

They sent guards to take him and put him into prison. He was accused of corruption. The charge was that he had invoiced the government for goods he had not taken delivery of, but the goods were on site and Edward could prove it. Instead of letting him go free however, they threw him into the death cell. Edward was terrified, as he knew people "disappeared" from this place.

During his interrogation the guards offered Edward some tea, but he heard God speak to him and tell him not to drink it, so he refused. "Who is your Godfather?" they asked him. "Jesus Christ and Him alone," he replied boldly. They jeered at him, realizing he had no Mafia protector.

They thought they could do whatever they wanted with him, but they were wrong. Edward did have a protector. Before the guards could force him to drink the poisoned tea, a higher official sent to have him released. The official said God had spoken to him and told him Edward was to be set free.

Upon his release, Edward fled the country and came to stay with relatives in England. He felt he had lost all that God had given him and all that he had worked for. It was a very low point, as he felt he had been robbed of the vision God had given him. Far from home and losing sight of God's purpose, he even reached the point of planning to commit suicide. But God had other plans.

Edward came to the Kingdom advice center in Guildford, where we prayed for him and prophesied over him. The prophecies reinforced the call of God upon him. What's more, the prophetic words said that the government of Ghana was going to change and that it would be safe for Edward to return then. God was going to bless him and his business. Edward continued attending the Kingdom advice center for about six months, growing in faith and understanding.

Prophecies Fulfilled

The prophecies started to be fulfilled. Against all the odds, the old Ghanaian government was toppled (together with the corrupt officials) and a Christian government put in its place exactly as had been prophesied. Edward felt safe to return and I went with him to encourage him. The situation did not look promising, however.

Some of the goods he had previously paid for had disappeared and Edward needed almost two million dollars to complete the project. The good news was that the word of God that had been prophesied over him at the Kingdom advice center said there would be a shortfall, but the government itself would settle that.

It was not easy going however, in spite of all the prophetic encouragement. The new government did not immediately release any money for the project, although it was agreed that they would. We went to visit the architect and found the approval to pay had not left his desk. Someone had tried to starve Edward out to cause him to default on his contract and incur large default payments.

Encouragement kept coming however. His mother rang and told him, "My Jesus is with you." His cousin rang and said, "The Lord has said some people are covering you in prayer. Put it before the courts and He will be the judge. Remember you are the apple of God's eye."

We all know we are the apple of God's eye, but at times it can be hard remembering that, especially when your business has gone belly up because of corruption, your life is under threat, and you can see bankruptcy looming. But Edward hung in there, believing the word of God.

During his time in England, it had been prophesied that there would be a court case that would bring some vindication for him, so Edward put his faith in God and His word to him. The hand of God was clear in the court case and Edward was vindicated, and the new government agreed to pay the almost two million dollar shortfall, as was prophesied.

Living in a Miracle

Now Edward is doing well. He is a living testimony to God's hand of protection for His workplace warriors. He says himself, "Miraculous events took place. And still prophetic words are being fulfilled. I am living in a miracle."

Where God calls, He provides. It can be challenging and it can be contrary to what you have expected. When things start to go wrong, pray and then pray harder, don't quit. But for most of us that doesn't come easily when we're facing these sorts of situations.

Edward is not the only one who thought he'd lost everything before God turned the situation around for him.

Workplace ministry is not an easy option, though many may think it is. It's a battleground where the stakes are high and the confrontations are real, and not everyone makes it through. The battle scars are deep and lasting, but oh, the rewards of running through with God!

Even after Gideon had encountered the Angel of God and taken the first step of obedience, he still needed confirmation about his calling. It seemed so preposterous that God should call an unknown young man from an insignificant family to do such a great work as freeing Israel, yet Gideon's heart yearned for freedom to be theirs.

Edward needed further confirmations also, especially when things were not going as expected and there was so much opposition. Just as with Gideon, God gave him those confirmations. There will be confirmations for those who are called, but sometimes even these take a form, or come at a time, we are not expecting.

God rescued Edward at his darkest hour. The last thing he expected when he came to England was to find a group of people who were hearing God speak about his life and calling into the business world in his home country of Ghana. He thought he was all washed up, but in a small town in the English countryside he discovered God was still on his case and that He was confirming His calling of him into the business arena where he had just failed so dramatically. And just as he found the grace of God was being poured out all over him, he came to know a new face of God, and to live in a deeper relationship with Him.

Personal vision carries personal challenges, but company challenge places even greater pressures on those who are called. Companies are like cities in the Bible: groups of people going about their daily work with different skills working together to benefit the whole. God has much to say in the Bible about the running of cities and His purposes for them. Today's companies are similar in size, and often even bigger, than those old biblical cities. So what are the challenges of running your company God's way? What are the challenges of finding God's divine purposes for your company and working with Him to fulfill them?

One man who has found out is Julian Watts. Intelligent, successful, leaving university with a double first in business and information technology, Julian carefully followed his career plans to success, until he came under the heavy hand of God and was brought down to the place where through testing and trials, God realigned his attitudes and helped him to become a mighty workplace warrior.

Career Plans Hijacked by the Lord's Vision

Julian thought he knew what God wanted him to do in life: be successful and bless his local church financially. He set out his 15-year plan to get where he wanted to be—a partner in a global strategy consulting firm—and went for it determinedly right from university. He built up his skills and career experience in business and information technology, then in strategy and consulting. Upon joining KPMG, one of the top four global accounting and consultancy firms, as a strategy consultant he worked with chairmen and chief executives of big multinational corporations and was made a partner right on time in his career plan. Then God stepped in.

Julian realized the Lord was calling him to leave the prestigious company he was in and walk out into the unknown. This was never part of his 15-year career plan! However, God's hand was persuasive. He discussed his conclusions with his pastor and wise friends, who all confirmed he was right in his thinking. God was calling him out.

Just when he thought his future was certain and he was set to have 25 prosperous and happy years as a partner, he found the hand of the Lord pressing on him. This was Julian's graduation test. Did he really believe God had his career in His hands or not? Would he miss God's calling and have a luxurious but unfulfilled life walking his own path?

Julian knew he had to turn his prospective future down and leave. He resigned his partnership with no idea of what to do, just trusting in God to open the right doors for him. He knew it was time to stick with God and believe He would show Himself real and active when it came to the crunch.

Julian decided to do a strategy project with himself as the subject; it was after all what he had been doing for KPMG, only on a different scale. So he set about considering what would reshape the world of consultancy in the future. He designed an Internet system to buy and sell consultancy, then widened it to be for any service, then widened it still further to include any product or service.

Soon he was looking at a matchmaking system that covered the whole global business-to-business economy. Any business that bought from, or sold to, another business could profit from the system and could connect to it if they could just switch on a personal computer. It took three months to grasp the global scale of the complete vision. The vision was half rational (the consultancy) and half inspirational (adapting it for all products and services).

Realizing the vast potential of this concept and being very aware of the spiritual element of what he was proposing, Julian sat down with God and asked why He wanted him to do this. The Lord revealed the first of several purposes He had for the company: releasing a percentage of global trade to finance the harvest of souls. So Julian set up a charitable trust to receive 10% of all gross company revenues, with the specific aim of paying for and equipping the Christian workers to bring in the end time harvest, and set out to operate the new company based on the principle of making lots of money and giving it to God.

However, even at this early stage the Lord had another surprise in store. Having called Julian to put all his savings from his years at KPMG into the new company, the Lord now made it clear to Julian and his wife that while it was fine to pay salaries to other people working in the company, He did not want Julian and his wife, as the founders, to draw a salary until the company had started to make donations to the charitable trust!

Living by faith was the one thing Julian had said to his wife he would never do, but now the Lord was calling them to do just that! Despite their initial fear and unbelief, they accepted out of obedience and started on a four-year journey that would lead them into complete dependency on the Lord for literally everything—food, clothes, mortgage for their home, everything.

During the most desperate times of this experience of living by faith—times when they literally had no money to buy food for the week or new shoes for their children—the Lord always faithfully provided somehow. And it was also during this same time that they would be led in obedience to the Lord to decline offers to purchase their company, valuing their shares at between US$50 million and US$75 million, as they recognized that selling it into non-Christian hands would destroy everything the Lord was doing through the company!

Boom Time

In 1999 the start-up company was growing rapidly as Julian built it up on a purely commercial basis. This was Internet boom time and the company, Markets Unlocked, moved from a home office to a small office, to a larger office, then to a huge office in London, which was used to take clients around a large exhibition on the company. Markets Unlocked was riding the Internet wave well.

It was during this time that Julian met me for the first time. As Julian says, "The Lord made it very clear to me that it was important that Richard joined Markets Unlocked, but it was only with the benefit of hindsight that I fully appreciated why. Before Richard joined we had no real concept that the Lord could be interested in a business for its own sake, rather than just as a vehicle to release finance for the Kingdom.

"The Lord made sure Richard was in place before He took us to the pivot point—the point where He broke us individually and as a company while paradoxically, at the same time showing us His passion for us individually and as a company. The Lord knew that we would need help moving to this new mindset and made sure that Richard was with us, coaching us through the transition. Then, once we had made the move and were walking forward in this new way, Richard's assignment from the Lord with us was complete and the Lord moved him on to his next challenge."

Richard sought advice before joining the company and arranged for Bishop Bill Hamon and Sharon Stone to meet with Julian. The prophetic word the Lord spoke through Bishop Hamon and Sharon Stone has been so accurate (approximately 90% of this detailed six-page prophecy has already been fulfilled!) that Markets Unlocked views it as one of two foundational prophecies over the company.

The Crash

The pivot point came with the dot-com crash in 2000, when all external funding stopped overnight. Julian knew that fulfilling his responsibilities as a director would require him to make some tough decisions. During that time, the Lord graciously gave Julian several confirmations of what he needed to do next by giving three people independently within a 48-hour period the same word for Julian about how the Lord had reduced Gideon's army.

This was the most traumatic point for Julian: most of the people in the company were personal contacts from his business, social and church worlds who were well-qualified for their roles in the company. They were already, or had now become, Julian's personal friends, but now he had no choice but to make them redundant. Having announced the situation to all of the staff, Julian went out of the room, slumped in the corridor utterly heartbroken, and wept silently.

At this darkest moment, the Lord was again gracious with Julian. As he was weeping, one of the staff he had just made redundant came out and told Julian that it had been a privilege working for him. Then two more people who had just been made redundant came out, helped Julian back to his office, and stayed to encourage him for the rest of the afternoon.

By the end of the following day, every member of staff who had been made redundant had been to see Julian, many bringing him flowers and gifts. In the months that followed, about half the people went back to doing the work they had been doing before, while for the others, the Lord used their time in the company as a stepping-stone to bring them into new roles, industries and levels of responsibility.

Despite the desperate situation now facing the business, Julian knew that the Lord was calling him to stay with the company. In addition, it was in the best interests of the creditors and external shareholders that the company trade its way out of difficulty even though it would involve great personal sacrifice by the directors. To Julian's amazement a number of the staff had also realized they were called to the company despite there being no funds to pay them and together they started to seek the Lord for His way forward.

Prayer Deepens

As things had been getting worse, the team started praying together, first monthly, then weekly and finally, as desperation set in, daily. Their prayers had just one focus: the list of things they required the Lord to do for them to sustain the business.

The more time Julian and the team spent with the Lord, the more the things they did during that time began to change. Gradually the list of urgent prayer requests gave way to simply worshipping Him—seeking His face rather than His hand. As they now had office space but considerably fewer staff, a room was set aside as a company prayer room. The corporate communications director no longer had much to communicate about and started spending more and more of her time in the prayer room, worshipping the Lord and praying for the company.

The more they simply worshipped, the more they saw the Lord intervene directly in the spirit realm and the earthly realm to sustain the business during the darkest, most desperate moments through the rest of 2000 and into 2001. Time after time, at the 11th hour, He would provide just what was needed and no more.

The staff's daily routines began to change. Julian started having his own personal time with the Lord from 5:00 A.M. to 7:00 A.M. each day. Then from 8:00 A.M. to 9:00 A.M., all the company directors would meet to worship and pray. From 9:00 A.M. to 2:00 P.M. every weekday, Liz Jones (the former corporate communications director who by now had been formally recognized as the intercessory director) worshipped and interceded for the company with her team. Every Tuesday from 10:00 A.M. to 12:00 P.M., everyone in the company would meet, along with local pastors and intercessors, to worship and intercede.

Sustained in the Wilderness

One of the best examples of the Lord's provision happened during this time. Julian had agreed to pay the creditors all off in three chunks at the end of December, January and February. This meant the company had to have the money in place by the Friday of Christmas Eve because of the Christmas holiday. The time got closer and closer but there was still no money.

On that Thursday morning, Julian provisionally agreed a financing deal to get through the first installment. There were lots of strings attached and Julian was very uneasy but could see no other way forward. During the afternoon several of the intercessors phoned independently to say they felt there was something wrong with the deal spiritually.

That evening Julian returned home to find his wife in tears. That day they had received a £10,000 tax demand relating to his time at KPMG, but as they were now living by faith they had no money to pay. It was the final straw—all Julian and his wife could do was sit and sob. Julian said to God, "Lord, I don't think this deal is right, but I have no other responsible option, so I'm going to have to go through with it tomorrow unless you can come up with an alternative while I'm asleep." Then he fell into bed completely exhausted and he slept.

During the night someone put £1,000 through their front door. (It subsequently turned out that the tax demand was massively overstated and the £1,000 they received that night covered almost all of the correct amount). Then at 4:00 A.M., Julian received a phone call from Australia from Warren Sinclair, the Markets Unlocked chief executive officer regarding the people who were negotiating for the Markets Unlocked national license in New Zealand.

The New Zealanders had felt prompted to send a payment through ahead of any paperwork. The money came through electronically and so later on the Friday morning of Christmas Eve, Julian was able to withdraw from the financing deal he was concerned about and spend the rest of the day writing checks to completely clear the first of the three installments. It was a defining moment. Julian had gone to bed with nothing, but in the night, while Julian slept, God did it all.

The Lord subsequently provided the funds to pay off the second installment and half of the third installment. Having miraculously cleared five-sixths of the debt in a matter of months, the Lord left the final one-sixth in place for a considerable period of time, ensuring that Julian and the company continued to live in complete dependency on Him.

The Lord Reveals His Blueprint for the Company

While the Lord was sustaining Markets Unlocked through the wilderness by a series of miraculous provisions, at the same time He also set about rebuilding every aspect of the business according to His blueprint. Two key areas in which He intervened directly were the business processes and organizational structure.

The Lord showed Julian that the process he had been following when establishing the business overseas was the opposite of how the Lord wanted it done in the future. Up until then, as Julian was primarily focused on the commercial aspects of the business, his process for establishing the company overseas was to meet with business people to set up the company while hoping that someone somewhere was praying for the company in that country and then waiting until the company was generating finances before establishing the charitable trust.

The Lord's approach was the other way around. Now when Julian establishes Markets Unlocked in another country (or at a state level in the USA) all he does on his first visit is meet with the national level apostolic leaders to share the vision of Markets Unlocked and formally ask for their welcome, blessing and cover, as the Lord showed him they have spiritual authority in the land.

Julian's second visit to a country focuses on meeting the national level intercessory network leaders—given what the Lord is doing through the company, the spiritual battle over Markets Unlocked is so intense that it is essential to ensure the intercessory cover is in place even as the business is being birthed in that country.

Only when the apostolic and intercessory cover is in place does Julian return for a third time to meet with the Christian business people—the Calebs with the calling, character, credibility and capability—to establish the Markets Unlocked company in their country.

As well as changing the core processes of the business, the Lord also directly intervened to change the organizational structure in a way that had major financial and legal implications. Julian was at his network of churches annual conference when the Lord took him through a very intense refining process that included him spending most of an afternoon flat on the floor of his hotel room before the Lord.

During this time, the first thing the Lord said to Julian was: "My relationship with you is more important than anything you will ever do for me." Having spent almost his entire career in a consultancy environment where personal value and worth was based solely on performance, when the Lord said that His relationship with Julian was more important than Julian's performance for Him, it was a life-changing moment.

The second thing the Lord said was that given His priority sequence of relationship before performance/activity, He therefore had the right to ask Julian to pick up a particular calling and then lay it down, pick up the next calling and then lay it down, etc. Julian nervously agreed.

The Lord then delivered the third statement. He told Julian He therefore had the right to ask Julian to create the company and now He also had the right to ask Julian to lay it down. It was the shock of this that took the whole afternoon to work through. Julian realized the Lord was telling him to lay the company down even though he had poured his whole life, all his family's finances, emotional energy, everything, in to Markets Unlocked.

Julian argued and protested to the Lord for hours until by the end of the afternoon he was just too exhausted to continue arguing any more and he simply gave up. Julian acknowledged that the Lord was the Boss and if He wanted Julian to give the company away or walk away then that is what he would do. Having given up fighting with the Lord, Julian went into deep grieving as his baby, the company, was dead, and he continued grieving through the evening, the next morning and into the next afternoon.

Then suddenly the Lord spoke again to say that now Julian had finally let go of the company, the Lord wanted Julian to pick it up again but in a fundamentally different way. Julian had recognized that the Lord wanted to work through Markets Unlocked to release a percentage of global trade to finance the harvest of souls.

Out of his desire to be a good steward and ensure none of the money went astray, Julian's solution was to own and control everything, so the international parent company owned the country subsidiaries. But the Lord's blueprint was different. In Julian's commercial model the role of the international parent company was to own, control and police the country subsidiaries.

Following the Lord's blueprint, the role of the international company was to envision, enable, serve and support the country companies. And rather than owning the country companies, the ownership was to be in the hands of local nationals, so they were now fellow workers in seeing the Markets Unlocked vision fulfilled, rather than subordinates.

This had huge financial and legal implications for Julian, but in obedience to the Lord he restructured the legal and financial basis of the business to come in line with the Lord's blueprint. As a result, Markets Unlocked is moving in the opposite spirit to how England has traded with other nations through the centuries.

Instead of the centuries-old "Empire mentality," where the objective was to grab all of the wealth and take it back to the U.K., Markets Unlocked is creating wealth through the local Markets Unlocked companies in each country, releasing it to the local Calebs and also out through the charitable trust to finance the harvest of souls in that country.

The Lord Hits the "Go" Button

Having completely remodeled the entire business, the Lord was then ready to unveil His strategy that would, according to a prophetic word He gave through Chuck Pierce, "cause the company to take off like a rocket, so that we would be struggling to keep up with the pace the Lord was setting." As a global matchmaking system connecting businesses in every industry sector and country, Markets Unlocked could have launched anywhere, and in fact, the original roll-out strategy had a carefully thought out sequence of countries. However the Lord had different priorities.

Before September 11, 2001, there were hundreds of overseas trade delegation visits to Israel every year. Since that date, there have been virtually none. Israeli business is in crisis and her economic survival is at stake. Through an intricate series of divine appointments, particularly involving Gunnar Olson, the founder of the International Christian Chambers of Commerce, Markets Unlocked was launched in Israel in November 2002 with the director generals of the main Israeli trade associations as the global mechanism by which Israeli companies can now connect with Christians in business around the world. In his speech at the media launch in Israel, Julian was also able to share the company's motivation for blessing Israel in such a practical way:

"So on behalf of Christians around the world I would like to take this opportunity to say to the people of Israel, that you are so loved. That your God has so touched our hearts with His love for you that we are here to serve you if you will allow us to do so. Markets Unlocked is given as a free gift to you from the Christian community around the world as an act of repentance and reconciliation for what has been done to you through the centuries in the name of Christianity, and as a practical expression of our love and support for you. We stand together with you at this difficult time, and we would like you to know that you are not alone."

Transforming Cities

The Lord promises to bless those who bless Israel and as Markets Unlocked, a company based in the city of Guildford, has started to bless Israel, the Lord has been blessing the city of Guildford in a very specific way.

As a city, Guildford is known for having one of the highest divorce rates in Europe and for its materialism, with many people commuting from the city to work in the head offices of major corporations and investment banks in central London. However, the Lord had spoken during a week-long prayer conference for Guildford that He was going to transform the city through the various spheres of society, starting with business and then youth, education, local government, etc.

As Liz Jones, the intercessory director, and the rest of the team at Markets Unlocked spent more time with the Lord, the more He drew them into the identity of all believers as part of the Bride of Christ. After some time they began to realize that the Lord was making this intimacy with Him as part of His Bride one of the defining characteristics of the company—that He was calling Markets Unlocked to be a company of the Bride.

As they hesitatingly stepped forward into this new identity, the Lord increasingly gave them a burden to intercede for their city and in one of the company prayer meetings, the Lord overwhelmed Julian with His heart for Guildford, prompting Julian to declare Isaiah 61: 10–62:5 over the city. The enemy had tried to destroy the city with a false identity of divorce and materialism, but the Lord had revealed His redemptive destiny for Guildford as a city of the Bride and storehouse to give to the nations!

A series of divine connections and events had resulted in the church leaders in Guildford inviting Julian to be part of their monthly leaders meeting as the only non-congregational Christian leader in the group. Julian therefore formally asked the church leaders to weigh and test whether this word for the city was from the Lord.

After a few days the leaders came back, confirming that this was the Lord's heart for the city and at the next cross-denominational meeting in the city they had Julian stand in front of the congregation and declare the scriptures from Isaiah over the city, calling Guildford into her true identity as a city of the Bride and breaking the power of the spiritual rulers and powers which had held the city for so long in her false identity of divorce and materialism.

The church leaders then arranged for Julian to share the testimony of the company in place of the sermon in the Sunday morning services in a number of churches in the city. Many people came forward at the end for ministry, with Liz Jones leading the churches' ministry teams in prayer for people, imparting the identity and intimacy as the Bride, and breaking the spiritual strongholds in people's lives. By the end of 2002, the church leaders had also arranged for Liz to minister at two other cross-denominational meetings as well as the prayer school, imparting intimacy and identity as the Bride. Shortly afterward the church leaders formally appointed Liz to the leadership group as the lead intercessor for the city.

By the beginning of 2003, the church leaders had concluded that the Lord's heart was to transform Guildford into the City of the Bride through the various spheres of society such as business, education, etc., thereby combining the destiny of Guildford as a city of the Bride with the prophetic word about transforming the city in sequence through the spheres of society.

The Results So Far

So where are we today in this journey of personal, corporate and city transformation? What are some of the tangible results Julian can see already emerging from all that the Lord has been doing?

"At a personal level, we have witnessed the Lord sustain our family without a salary for almost four years. This new experience of a faithful heavenly Dad, combined with a growing intimacy with Jesus as part of His Bride, and increasing friendship with the Holy Spirit has transformed the Christian lives of my wife and I and resulted in each of our three children becoming Christians within in the last two years.

"At a corporate level, following the Lord's blueprint rather than man's best strategy has resulted in Markets Unlocked now being used by companies in more than 50 countries around the world to find new customers or better suppliers. In addition, the Lord is also now working through Markets Unlocked to: bless Israel by connecting Israeli companies with Christians in business around the world; help the poor and needy by connecting companies with excess products and services with charities which distribute to the needy; and release a percentage of global trade to finance the harvest by charging a small fee to connect business buyers with business suppliers in any industry and country in the world.

"Finally, in terms of transforming Guildford into the city of the Bride, the church leaders are currently planning a week of prayer with each day focussing on a different sphere, and then in a weekend event is being planned where congregations across the city will all meet together in response to the Lord's call for Guildford to walk in her redemptive destiny as a city of the Bride."

The Waste Howling Wilderness

It's when we have to walk the stuff out that we find what really we're made of. It's as we take head-on all that satan has to throw at God's vision, be it for a man or a company, that we develop a new understanding of who God is, His Grace and our utter dependence on Him in every way. He and He alone can cause the fulfillment of His visions.

We discover in a new and deeper way that only when we are safely tucked up in Him, like a baby kangaroo in its mother's pouch, are we able to walk forward on the right path. God will not be manipulated for our own ends, but marches on to fulfill His purpose through us.

Walking out our call is a continuous process, so we need to recognize where we are in that process and start to work with God to get to the place He wants us to be. In Deuteronomy 32:10 it say,

> *He found him in a desert land, And in the howling waste of a wilderness; He encircled him, He cared for him, He guarded him as the pupil of His eye.* (NASB)

It may seem hard going at times, as both Edward and Julian's stories show, but they also show how closely God is present with us. He is teaching us, tending us, caring for us in extraordinary ways. God's lessons may seem hard for us to learn because so often they are contrary to worldly wisdom or the world's perceived well-being for us as individuals.

But He is our best instructor. He places people alongside us to help us, He opens our eyes to our own insecurities, and He resolutely stands against anything that comes against a steady deepening of our relationship with Him.

In Egypt, the Israelites were abused, oppressed and poor. In the wilderness, they were victorious in battle, had plenty to eat, and their clothes and shoes did not wear out. They were in a place of victory and plenty. God led them by the pillars of cloud and fire. Foreign kings honored them as victors. That's how God takes us and makes us victors in our given field.

Of course we first have to discover our field or sphere, but then we have to walk out our calling in the gifts He has given us for the purpose He has called us, and in His timing. It means listening to Him closely, seeking Him at every point to determine what stage of strategy we are in, what weapons we are to use to fight each battle, and how we are to open ourselves to His refinement of our hearts until we more closely resemble Him and reveal Him to others.

After our glorious encounter with Him when we discover our calling, our times in the wilderness are times of growing intimacy with our God, growing understanding of how to trust Him with all that is most precious to us, growing dependence on Him, and times of mounting victory. But they are wilderness times and there can be times when life seems very bleak.

For Edward in the death cell in prison, it was a real wilderness place, but God showed Himself to be with him and saved him. For Julian and his wife sobbing together in shock as they faced an empty bank account, an outrageous tax demand and the mortgage and creditors looming, it was a very real wilderness place, but in the night God proved Himself strong and there for them. He proved Himself Jehovah Jireh, the God who provides for us. We need those times when we are up against the wall, to find out for ourselves that He is with us in all the practical matters as well as the spiritual.

Gideon encountered God and heard Him call him forth in that name, *"mighty warrior,"* and he developed a new vision of himself. So today, as we encounter God's calling of us and deepen our relationship with him, we grow in understanding of who we are in Him. As we catch the vision He has implanted in us, we grasp hold of the fact that we can do it. Others may not see it in us, but when God has called, it runs deep and the calling is hard to kill. But visions evolve as Julian's story shows, and as faith and dependence grew in him, he discovered more and more aspects of God's wider calling of him and his company and the unfolding purposes of God in his life.

Corporation Vision

During my time working alongside Julian, God started to bring a strong revelation about different levels of working with His Word. One level is for us as an individual and a family, but there is also another level for an organization, corporation, city or nation. Of course all the principles of individual and family hold good for the corporation, city and nation. They are not different principles. The walls that are broken down in an individual or a family are the same as the walls being broken down in a corporation. And when the walls are broken down, spirits that come in and out of people and families to kill, steal and destroy, also happen in corporations.

As God views a company as an individual entity, then we should be asking what is a godly corporation and what is any other corporation. All vision emanates from the third heaven and if God releases vision to a pulpit minister, He can release vision to a corporation minister, just as He can to people for a city or a nation.

He reveals vision, for He has plans and desires for every corporation, every structure. Once He releases vision, then all of the opposing forces that come against an individual or family, come against that corporation, city or nation. I think the next wave of book and magazine article releases we'll be seeing soon are going to be about spirits in the corporation. The enemy is coming to kill, steal and destroy the corporation with all of his schemes and scams as if it was a living person.

All of those who are called as company or corporation visionaries come under a circumcising that is like they've never experienced anywhere else. Just as the Lord has been working through Julian's trials and tribulations as the refining fire, He has also been refining the team.

For most Christians in the workplace, their vision is to see themselves as the financial division for God. They think they will make money in the world the world's way and somehow give it to the local church for it to be put to heavenly use. They think if they give 10% of their income to the Kingdom, God will bless their worldly behavior.

Yet they won't impact the structure of the world; they won't even let them know they are Christians. "Don't let the shareholders or the stakeholders in the company know we're Christian or it'll stop us from earning the world's money." That's where the bulk of the world's Christians in the workplace/marketplace are.

But in Daniel 7:27, God says:

All the Kingdoms in the world are mine and I've given them to the saints. (Author's paraphrase.)

That's every kingdom that is currently in the world. They are given to us so we can turn them to God's agenda. We are the agents of change He uses.

Death and Resurrection

I have worked alongside several visionaries, most of whom, but not all, have finally succeeded in bringing themselves and their attitudes in line with God's thinking and their visions through the early stages of fulfillment. In every case, as with Edward and Julian, God's supernatural working to bring provision through the desert days has been awesome.

One of the most telling times was with Channel 7, a Christian television station. This was an example of taking a vision from God, getting it in order and God causing it, when it looked like it was dead, to rise and become the success He had always destined it to be.

One of God's visionaries had a vision to establish a television channel. He called it Channel 7. Channel 7 was struggling and finally reached the place where it was more than £1 million in debt. At that point I became a director and pulled it off the air. Then with lawyers and accountants we constructed Newco, a new company, and put together a Christian board with a new managing director.

After several months the new managing director and the board wanted to get rid of the visionary, but I could not support that. God has strong feelings for His visionaries; He won't let them be touched by anyone but Himself. He anoints, leads, purifies and protects them. For example, the people who came against one of God's biblical visionaries, Moses, variously got leprosy, were consumed by fire, the ground opened up and swallowed them, or they died by the plague!

Moses was leading a rag-tag group of people in a corporate movement from Egypt to a promised land, and along the way his own family, the priesthood and the people came against him. Moses' behavior was to hit the ground fast and say, "God, what do You want to do about this?" God's responses clearly showed where He stood on the matter. Christians should be careful of touching other Christian visionaries. I certainly had no intention of doing so without a very clear direction from the Lord.

This coup was not supported and that night the 35 staff of Channel 7 was reduced to two directors and two staff. Not long after that the Lord asked me to become managing director. After many awkward company losses I was earnestly seeking the Lord as to what degree a managing director under a visionary had the opportunity to determine the day-to-day implementation of the vision. Does the visionary have to have all of the authority of running a vision?

The Lord spoke to me through Moses building the tabernacle and the Lord appointing Bezalel and Aholiab in Exodus 31 to help him. Exodus 31:3 says:

> *...and I the Lord have filled him with the Spirit of God, in wisdom and ability, in understanding and intelligence, and in knowledge, and in all kinds of craftsmanship.*

My understanding was that God had the visionary Moses but He also appointed the other people to carry out this particular work of building the temple. God chose them and filled them with the wisdom and ability needed for the task.

It is so very important that God's visionaries are hearing Him correctly and are content to pass on their vision to others to administer if God is calling them to do so. In some cases, as in this one, that is what happens.

In most others, as in Julian's case, it is the visionary themselves who are called to administer the implementation of the vision through its inception to a fully functional reality. Hearing God and staying close to where He alone is taking us is of paramount importance. It is, of course, necessary for every one of us, but doubly so for the Lord's visionaries, as for them the stakes are higher.

At that point I started to take the role of the day-to-day administration of the implementation of the vision and bring it into what we believed was alignment. Channel 7 ended up with no property, no paid staff, no volunteer staff, no telephones, no bank account and no address. The thieves in the building used for short-term storage picked over the flesh and bones of the channel like vultures and took the unclaimed equipment. That was July 1999. By the 22nd of August that year even the visionary's prospectus, which we had financed to the tune of £25,000, was considered failed. For all intents and purposes, the vision, and Channel 7, were dead.

Then Terry Hickey from Trinity Broadcasting in the States rang and said, "We've got sponsorship of $150,000 a month, can you get us up on air?" God supernaturally got us prime time television from 6:00 P.M. to 12:00 A.M., for $140,000 per month. So for the first time in the channel's history there was a $10,000 surplus over the revenue to the expense of being on air.

That surplus went to pay the two staff members who had been around and working for no pay all the time. They started work on the channel and by the 3rd of September, God had the channel on air six hours a day. Not just on air, but on an analogue transponder, the most expensive transponder at that time. So something that was for all intents and purposes, dead, got up and walked like Lazarus ten days later.

The transponder contract was on a 30-day revolving notice because the vendors were really looking for somebody to buy it at a cost of $3.75 million per year for five years. We were using the prime viewing time and we were able to do that until November. Then a buyer came when one of America's biggest shopping channels wanted to buy the transponder.

They pre-empted some of our airtime to do test marketing, liked the response, and pitched to buy the channel in November. That would have killed off Channel 7, but God wasn't having that. He put us in the position to negotiate for the contract, but we had to find a $21 million guarantee for the five-year lease of the transponder, which of course we did not have.

In the meantime, God had taken Paul Crouch, the leading visionary at TBN, to Israel with a party of TBN partners. Every place they went, his lawyer's office, his driver's house, the local people said to him, "Come and see TBN on in the Middle East." He would ring us up in England, excited about the coverage in the Middle East. I had to say to him that it would not continue very much longer because we could not find the $21 million necessary to win the contract above the shopping channel.

When he heard this he got in a plane, flew to London and we picked him up and brought him to Channel 7, where we went through everything with him and he undertook the guarantee and the cost of paying in excess of twenty million dollars over several years.

That was December of 1999. By February of 2000 we were on 17 hours a day and by April, 24 hours a day. Today it is breaking even and transmitting from Spain. The signal goes from Moscow down through Eastern, Central and Southern Europe, the Mediterranean, across the Middle East and on to the tips of Africa and Asia.

God Achieves His visions His Way

In Channel 7 and both Edward's and Julian's stories, God proved that He is the One who provides when there is no provision. In all three stories, God resurrected the vision or company from the dead. Many times when a God-given vision appears to die it is God who has brought it to that place of near asphyxia. God refines and hones His vision and visionaries in His time, not ours, and often when it seems like commercial suicide. But His hand brings His purpose to fulfillment and His visionaries pass through the waters changed, but unscathed.

Isaiah 43:2 says,

When you pass through the waters, I will be with you, and through the rivers, they will not overwhelm you. When you walk through the fire, you will not be burned or scorched, nor will the flame kindle upon you.

How much more can we be assured that when it's God who has deliberately put us into the strong waters, He will sustain us and bring us safely home.

Visionaries have to remember that when Joshua confronted the Angel of the Lord outside Jericho and asked whose side He was on, that He answered that He was on no man's side, *but as Prince of the Lord's host have I now come* (see Josh. 5:14).

It is the same with those who carry God's vision through to fulfillment. They find out that God is not on what they had regarded as their side, but rather He is with them to fulfill His own purpose. If their purpose is mixed with human perspectives such as hoping for riches and success, they often find that God is speedily eliminating that from their hearts and giving them His own perspective on their situation.

The World's Best Versus God's Plan

Julian said he wanted the best to achieve God's vision. But at that point he was thinking of doing it the world's way, assuming that would also be God's way. That is how most expect they should act to honor God. But God's way and the world's way are usually fundamentally different.

In order to test and improve our commercial strategy, we met for a day with some of the world's leading Internet consultants. It was an expensive exercise but it confirmed that the worldly strategy the company was following at that point reflected the best of man's thinking so the company continued for some time down that path.

However, it was not God's strategy. While Julian was comfortable asking consultants for their best view, at that point he did not expect that God would answer him if he asked God for His view on what the strategy should be for the company.

For most people, the idea of asking God what to do and expecting Him to tell us directly is a foreign one. Their only concept of prophecy is prophesying into the unknown; most people have little idea of "prophetic counsel," which is simply prophesying into the known.

Like all of us, Julian kept his old value systems in place until God brought him to the end of himself. Then God got hold of his brokenness and rid him of his foreign gods and foreign thinking. It's only when we come to that place that God can really use us.

Between April and August, Julian's board of directors, all good Christians, went from the point of "why would the Lord be interested in our commercial strategy?" to having one-third of their remaining office space turned over to prayer, intercession and worship as they sought the Lord's direction for the way forward.

These are the different dynamics of what is a God-given vision for a corporation and of somebody just walking out their gifts and calling and making a load of money and giving it to God. When God gives vision, it is for one of His building blocks in the building of the Church in a city or a nation.

Another of the Lord's strategies we questioned was to license the Markets Unlocked concepts to nations before we even had a working model. To franchise a concept the worldly way is to build a model and prove that it works. Then you build a few more company owned ones, record the profit and loss, and set it up as a model. Only then do you go and sell it to people.

When the direction first came up of licenses and franchises, Julian naturally said it wouldn't work. There was nothing we could show people for them to make a rational judgment on before they committed to buy it. Although that's logical in our worldly thinking, when God steps in with His plans we find ourselves stepping out of the logical into the supernatural. There is no physical means of supporting a concept of licensing something to countries for a fee, which has not been proved to work or make a profit in practice.

But once we had accepted God's way, we began to find people who were interested in it. To then offer the use of the system free to Israel was another illogical step in the world's eyes, but God is more interested in His long-term agenda and in our obedience than He is in sustaining worldly logic.

Now Julian has been featured in the Israeli media and Christians in business in more than 50 countries are now using Markets Unlocked to trade with each other, with Israeli companies and with secular companies. That doesn't make any sense to the world.

I believe we are going to see companies and organizations being sustained by the word of His power and I believe we are going to see cities and whole nations upheld by the word of His power alone. Markets Unlocked is one prototype of that.

Changing Our Worldview

Most Christians I've spoken to start from a place where they think if they just do the bit that God wants them to do, then they can do well for themselves too. They imagine they will give 10% of the company profits or turnover to whatever God wants and keep the rest for themselves. It is all clear-cut and very simple.

Certainly God does have some of those people whose primary calling is to be a righteous personal witness in the workplace, and God prospers them. Basically they make a bunch of money just working the world's way, and God blesses it and somehow cleanses it and puts it over into the Kingdom. But it doesn't have any concept of God's vision or of God building the Church. Visionaries like Julian are called wider than that.

We also prophesied to Julian that all of the people who took up the franchises and who worked for him would be like different fields of trade. The legal profession would have their bit, the trading profession would have their bit, local government would have their bit, etc., with millions of Christians talking to each other across a vast area.

God has created such opportunity for His purpose through this initiative. Julian was unwittingly putting together an electronic structure of a workplace church that will put in a communications vehicle, like global television where each program is a message. Now when Julian and Liz, the intercessory director, stand up at conventions, motivating and encouraging the global body with their testimony, they are really sharing God's revealed patterns and principles, and God's character, to all of the people.

God is creating a movement through this vision. The financial development of this is not God's main concern. He doesn't need our money; He is more interested in building His Church and changing the world.

This is what happens when somebody is carrying a God-given vision. God cleans it, purifies it, adjusts motive and brings all kinds of refining that doesn't happen in a company that is just a worldly financial producer. You might think that if billions of dollars poured into the existing systems, it would build the Church. But it doesn't because it pours into the local church and the local church doesn't take over the world's management systems and therefore cannot on its own transform a city or a nation.

As Psalm 24:1 says,

> *THE EARTH is the Lord's, and the fullness of it, the world* (all the management systems of the inhabited world,) *and they who dwell in it.* (Explanation added by theAuthor.)

The word "*world*" part suggests that God is interested in the inhabited places (hyperbolically) the kingdom of Babylon, hence the control structures and management systems of a city, which is comprised of lots of corporations and organizations. He has vision for all of those.

It is one thing for an individual to be developing their gifts and finding their destiny, and it is quite another for one whom already knows their vision, has crossed their Jordan and is operating in their God-given field. God's dealings with His visionaries are different. Julian was a good student as he learned to depend upon God. He has passed the tests. As the vision is now becoming successful and he's ministering to many people, God is turning him into a proactive warrior and teaching him how to cope at the next level. That's the way it is for us all because it's a process.

It's all captured in Deuteronomy 32:10, 13:

He found him in a desert land, And in the howling waste of a wilderness; He encircled him, He cared for him, He guarded him as the pupil of His eye.... He made him ride on the high places of the earth... (NASB)

Part of making Julian ride in the high places is what he has been going through. God has *made* Julian ride in the high places whether he liked it or not. And through it all God has been purifying his heart and his motives.

Now the Lord has a man for His purpose. None of us can fly with God until we have allowed Him to form us as He wants us, and that means a process of refining and testing and purifying of our motives and our heart for Him. Nobody likes the refiner's fire, but we all have to go there if we are to fulfill the purposes God has for us.

Learning and Growth

God prospers His children abundantly, but I don't mean to suggest that if we have a workplace calling everything will be easy. Come to Him and everything will be fine and in the process you will be refined as pure gold. Jesus said, *"Take My yoke and learn of me."* As I see it, the length of duration of the hurt and pain is all to do with how quickly we roll over and die. Some of us are slow learners.

There's also another dimension and that's the size of the vision and the degree to which you are a forerunner. In this aspect, Julian is a forerunner because he's doing a global prototype. It's not a little deal; it's a global vision. Julian has been learning from the Lord and the degree of purifying that's going on is capable of sustaining a global vision.

Gideon grasped hold of the call of God and blew the trumpet in Zion, and the people rose up to do battle. But God whittled down those who were not alert to the tricks of the enemy and sent home those who were afraid, until Gideon's army had so few in it that only the mighty hand of the Lord could bring the victory.

So today God is raising up His "Gideon's army" of workplace warriors, refining them and putting them into places where only His mighty arm can bring them through to victory. He's firing them up with His vision, calling them to doggedly pursue His purpose, ravishing their hearts with love of His person, and bringing them to a place of utter dependence on Him.

Winning through to worldly success is not what matters in this battle, for that lies in His hand alone; but striking out into the middle of Ezekiel's river and running the race through with Him is what He wants from us.

And as we do, He hovers attentively over us, breathing on us and progressively forming His own image in us. To fight alongside the Lord to bring His purposes to pass; to help in His work of ushering in a "new thing"; to prepare the world for the second coming of the risen Christ—this is the awesome honor God bestows on His workplace visionaries.

CHAPTER 3

City Transformation– Dream of Reality

City Transformation: Dream or Reality?

It has become evident over years of faithful work, that evangelism projects alone do not transform a city. Recently, prayer has poured into the heart of cities to affect transformation, but although transformation cannot be effected without prayer, prayer alone cannot do it either. As the Church pushes forward with evangelism and prayer initiatives, the sad truth is that our cities remain largely untouched by the gospel.

We cannot and should not expect any city to be totally and permanently transformed until the culture of the structures and organizations within it have also been transformed. The companies and institutions that make up a city need to be taken out of Babylon and brought into the Kingdom.

So how is this city transformation enacted? How can the health service, the police force, the banks and the commercial conglomerates be transferred from Babylon to the Kingdom where Jesus is Lord? How can the ghettos be brought out of their deprivation into the prosperity Jesus promises to all? Not only how can it be done, but also what will it look like?

Jesus Is the Answer

Part of my understanding of the answer to that question came to me in a series of visions when I was in a prayer meeting in Sunderland led by Lois Gott. The first vision came flying at me out of a television set, so real that I involuntarily ducked. The words, "Jesus is the answer," just kept coming at me. It was a weird experience, but very vivid. Then it changed and became like the time exposure postcards that you sometimes see in London, with car lights pictured as scrawled red and yellow lines down the roads.

I heard the Lord saying, "These lines are depicting all the people I'm sending to every element of a functioning city, to all the workplaces, carrying the baton of what I want them to do." I knew they were people going in and out of buildings saying, "Jesus is the answer." It was as if the whole city of London was just whizzing around at this fantastic pace with people going into all these places because Jesus was their only answer.

Then the scene changed and I was flying like an eagle up the highway. As you go north and over the hills you'll suddenly see down in the valley millions of yellow lights. But as I was flying I saw some red neon lights too. Not many, but enough to be significant. Flying nearer to these red lights I could see the signs reading, "Jesus is the answer."

They were attached to all manner of buildings across the city. And as I flew I sensed a terrible black murkiness at the street level. It was filthy and dirty and hopeless and everywhere it was dark. But in the doorways of the buildings that had the red neon "Jesus is the answer" lights on them, hands were coming from the light inside, stretching out into the black and pulling people into the building where they could be safe.

Running on the Spot

That event was in 1996 and it helped me understand another strange experience I had two years earlier. Rodney Howard Browne came to the country and I was consumed by the Holy Spirit—running on the spot with my hands in the air and shouting, "in here, it's safe in here, in here, Jesus is the answer, in here." Night after night I'd go on like that, running on the spot and shouting out the same thing. I was sweaty, tired and feeling stupid, but God did not let up on me.

At the time, nobody understood behavior like that, as we hadn't seen it before. But when I saw these visions in Sunderland, it hit me that what I'd been doing back in 1994 was running to all these buildings with their red neon lights in all these cities saying, "in here, in here, Jesus is the answer, it's safe in here, Jesus is the answer."

It was at that point God said to me, "Son, I'm raising up marketplace apostles, corporate apostles, and they are coming to take back every element of a functioning city that has been counterfeited by the world and largely abdicated by the Church. And I want you to get up alongside them, work with them and help them walk out the plan I've given them. Help them to work with me and understand My character. Create training centers where they can come and learn."

Turnover, Profit and Heart

From there He took me into Matthew 25:31-46 about judging the sheep and the goats, talking about giving those in need a drink of water, food, etc. I extracted it out to see what it would look like in a city and arrived at a hope for the future, where companies acted on their Kingdom responsibilities to the communities around them.

I saw local people being saved and dragged out of poverty and hopelessness into Kingdom joy and riches. He showed me how He would fund it all. Instead of appealing for funds to come into a local temple, He would resource millions as a percentage of the "Jesus is the answer" organizations. And He would give them the turnover, profit and heart to handle those two dimensions of evangelism and provision.

I saw that anybody could come to their door in hopelessness and desperation and there would be hands that could pull them in there and provide for them. Together with experienced prophets Sharon Stone and Bill Hamon, I worked with these visions to put them onto paper to bring a practical outworking. It was my first concept diagram, the Hopper Diagram.

Figure 1—Hopper Diagram

So, how in practical terms can such a lavish vision be realized, particularly since it runs against the perceived wisdom of our age? The answer is for the actual environmental climate and internal culture of those organizations to change. We need a Kingdom mindset change across the organizations, cities and nations.

Visionary Spheres

Currently, most Christians' experience of the workplace is that they do their work to the best of their ability, without greatly impacting their colleagues with their faith. Even in the case of gifted evangelists, they often have little real fruit in their workplaces to show for all their effort. The Babylonian environment around them shows little or no change for their presence there. A kind of acceptance is achieved. Don't put your faith in my face and I won't force mine on you.

Here in this diagram, we see the Christian light trying to impact the word about it, but the heavy force of Babylon is pushing back, and through weight of numbers, tends to be in the majority. Very quickly a status quo is established. This is the Christian walking out their gifts and callings in the workplace. They may be successful and make money, and they may convert a few people to Jesus, but they are not bringing Kingdom rule into their workplace enough to change the spiritual atmosphere of the environment. They are not bringing a habitation of the land. They are not enforcing the dominion spoken of in Genesis 1:28. This is a position of training and preparation. It is not the fullness of calling for anyone.

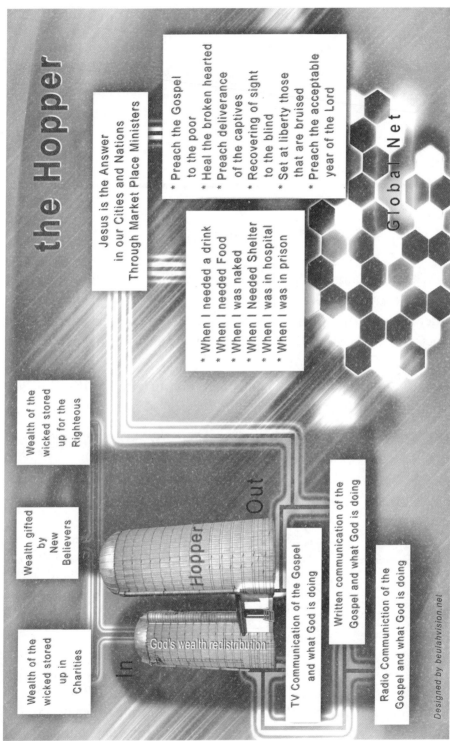

Figure 1 - Hopper Diagram

Figure 2—Diagram of Average Christian Workplace Experience

When the Christian hits, either by stumbling across it or by direct revelation, upon God's strategy for their workplace though, the picture is different. Here the light erupts into the workplace and affects many others, in some cases filtering through the whole company.

Figure 3—Diagram of Workplace Experience With God's Strategies in Place

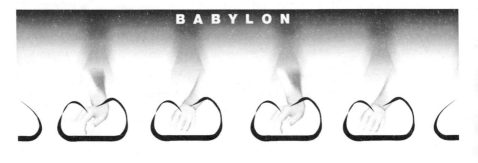

Although Babylon still keeps pushing back, the implementation of God's strategy for habitation and dominion through filling the land with people of His Spirit, provides the force to break open even the most closed environment. When we implement God's strategies it always draws upon His power from heaven into that situation. Intercessors know this, but for some reason many workplace warriors have not yet grasped hold of its significance. So they continue working Babylon's way.

Implementing God's Strategy

When we do enter a company with God's strategy, the effects can be far reaching. They can affect the life of a department, or even the whole company. Arthur Burk is one example of a man who proved God in this.

Back into Plumbing

Arthur Burk, of the trailblazing Plumbline Ministries, was sent by God back into the construction industry in the U.S. to demonstrate God's strategy and its effectiveness. Although Arthur had been given powerful revelation by God about the redemptive gifts of cities and was already working to awaken the Body of Christ to this new mindset, he felt God calling him out of his traveling ministry to go back into plumbing.

The background for his experience is a very familiar passage in Jeremiah 29:7, whose promise is very simple: seek the peace and prosperity of the city to which I have carried you into exile and pray to the Lord for it because if it prospers so will you. That promise was given to the people of Judah who were taken into exile in Babylon, which means they were a minority and an economically disadvantaged people who had no civil rights.

Yet God said to the prisoners of war who were living in a ghetto, that if this minority would pray for the peace and prosperity of their community, it would be so transformed that it would trickle down, even to their level. The ghetto is the last place where improvements in a culture actually arrive.

The concept of one man changing the prosperity of a company just through prayer cuts right across the traditional American cultural mindset that says you need large quantities of people to affect change. It was a pretty politically incorrect thing for God to do.

For the Lord to pull Arthur out of a ministry that was gratifying to him and beneficial to the Body of Christ, and send him back to construction, a fairly dishonored trade in the States, went against the expectations of many people. But Arthur felt he had heard the Lord, so he made the decision.

Going back into the plumbing trade after he had been out of it for several years could have been difficult, but he found someone who was willing to hire him. This man was a second-generation plumber who knew his plumbing well, but he was not a very successful businessman.

He had been in his current business for six years and had only achieved a gross annual income of $250,000 for the entire business. Not much, particularly for the plumbing industry, which is dominated by robber barons who abuse their power. Arthur went in as a journeyman plumber, but he was the new guy in the company with no seniority. He had no authority, and wasn't running a crew or given responsibility over anybody.

The boss did not hire him because he was a Christian. He never expressed any interest or approval of anything of a Christian nature. He was not seeking God, nor did he welcome or endorse any of Arthur's Christianity. He hired him in spite of the fact that he had some testy religious tendencies; he hired him to do plumbing. During the whole time he was there Arthur made few overtly spiritual moves and they were all roundly dismissed whether he was dealing with other employees or with the boss.

Arthur set out to be a good plumber and to engage in spiritual warfare on behalf of his company. He prayed blessing for his boss and the company, and pushed back the darkness in very specific ways. Arthur believes that if you are doing spiritual warfare, you ought to be able to get results which are measurable, verifiable and sustained, and that's what he was looking for in this new assignment God had given him.

One-Year Results

One year after he started working as a junior plumber, the company had gone from a $250,000 turnover to $750,000. The boss had not changed his business practices. Being an unbeliever he was still violating God's principles and he was reaping the natural consequences of those violations. Yet in spite of the devouring that was going on as a natural consequence of his sin, the blessings that God bought into the company by Arthur's presence and prayers transcended that devouring natural law. So from the boss's point of view, the company was blessed financially.

There was a complete turnover of employees during the time Arthur was there and the new expanded crew that was hired had better quality people than those who had been working there before. Personally Arthur also experienced the blessing of Jeremiah. He started at $18 an hour, and one year later was making $25 an hour. That is a staggering raise in one year in any industry.

Then, 14 months later the final release came. Arthur was putting in a shower valve for a widow. He was not being the least bit spiritual. He was not seeking God about leaving the company. But God spoke to him completely out of context, and very directly, and said, "You can leave plumbing now, I will provide for you financially." There had been no inkling that was coming that day; it was just two sentences out of the blue, clearly spoken by God into his mind. So he handed in his notice and prepared for his next assignment from the Lord.

Mostly Arthur had prayed blessing over the company and employees, but there were specific times of spiritual warfare too. One example of such a time was when a new girl who brought with her a strong victim spirit started working in the office. The devouring of her life in terms of her car being stolen and her landlord cheating her and her boyfriend problems was just astounding.

The day she started working in the office, that devouring spirit of victimization was released over the entire company. Nobody was able to complete a job, from the boss down to Arthur. Tools and parts were missing and customers changed their minds. Every plumber has a day like that periodically, but on this occasion the entire company was affected. The next day they went back out and tried again, but it was the same.

Arthur realized as he sought the Lord that it was demonic, not just a bad day for everybody. And as he began to target her, he explained to her demons that although they had a legal right to her because of her sin, and because she had invited them in, he had spiritual jurisdiction over the company. Therefore, as long as she was in the company they were to be inactive and not harass her. Instantly the difficulties in the company stopped.

That poor girl was still abused by the demons from the minute she left the office until she came back each morning, but she was blessed and protected inside the company. With that problem solved, Arthur continued to pray blessing over his boss and the other plumbers, none of whom deserved it, none of whom appreciated it or asked for it or ever acknowledged that the blessings were the result of God's intervention. But he did it nonetheless, and through him, God proved that He is still the God of the remnant.

Throughout his time with the company, Arthur was emphatically not in a position to influence the marketability of the company. He was not in any leadership position, was not in sales, and the major new contracts that his boss was offered he had never been offered before. The tangible effect of his intangible prayers was that the company he was blessing was offered contracts that would normally have gone to bigger plumbing companies. They also made a profit on some huge jobs that were way over their heads and that they could have lost a lot of money on.

Arthur's ministry in city-reaching and many other contexts has almost invariably revolved around a handful of people who get results hugely disproportionate to their numbers because they are willing to back everything on God's principles. This is only one illustration of where Arthur had staked his life on the validity of God's strategies.

Arthur was God's man for the moment in that company. He became a small area of influence that significantly affected the welfare of that company because he was implementing God's strategies. He was not building a habitation for the Kingdom to come, but he was implementing God's strategy and affecting the overall prosperity and quality of the company staff. If he had been called to stay in the company longer, God would probably have given him a strategy that would have affected the company employees in other ways and prepared the way for Kingdom advance in that place.

God Always Has His Man Ready

If a secular company can be transformed financially and its quality of staff significantly improved in one year, how long does it take to transform a city? There's more to transformation than increased financial prosperity, though that is always part of it. The very thought of city transformation is exciting. It is right at the center of the heart of God's purpose for our nations. But how does God transform a city? How does He work to transform the structures within it? As always, God works according to the principles He has established in His Word. He works through man and God always has His man ready for the job.

Arthur Burk's story shows how God can use a man to change a company through His strategy. But God's strategies are all different. He changes companies in many ways. A strategy can often be a short-term initiative, as in Arthur's case. But God also uses longer-term strategies. We call them visions, and they are released to God's visionaries.

Men and women of God can carry and implement His longer-term strategies for bringing His Kingdom rule into their environment. That can be at work, in a family or small group situation, or in a community. When God imparts vision, it always has to do with His purposes for that person and for that territory. Wherever you are, that is what God is speaking into. The person becomes a unit of transformation within their environment. I call that unit a "sphere" of transformational function.

Vision from God is always supernatural and always comes by revelation in the first instance. Visions from God can never be achieved by our own strength and planning; the visionary always has to call God's power into his situation to fulfill the dream.

The Sphere—The Smallest Unit of Change

So how does a "sphere" of transformation function at a company level? God gives vision to His man for His purpose within that person's sphere of influence. In any given organization, there will be many spheres of operation, all interacting. For example, there will be a financial sphere led by a financial specialist who has a vision from God as to how He wants to transform the finance division of the company.

God's man brings in Kingdom ethics and values and His power in miracles, prosperity, healings and the outworking of His will to change mindsets in that environment. There also will be different departmental spheres, all concentrating on their differing functions within their area of the company, but all separately envisioned by the Holy Spirit for transformation.

Within these spheres of operation, the visionaries gather around themselves people who can identify with the vision and often have a real sense of calling to that vision, as we saw in the examples of the God Channel and Markets Unlocked. These people are separately and individually called by God to be part of the team that sees through the vision. This is their sphere of function.

They are shining the light of the Kingdom into that department as they work to fulfill the vision God has given them. They are chosen and gifted for their task by God's hand, as we see in Exodus 31:1-11, where God anointed Bezalel and Aholiab in Moses' day, to build and decorate the ark and the tent of God's presence.

God values His visionary spheres highly. He imparts short and longer-term plans and purposes to them and provides the motivation to keep them at it, no matter what comes at them, along with all the resources they need to fulfill their function. Then He carries the risk for them. Spheres are a highly charged unit of transformation. Within a company there could be several spheres, but all are of equal value in His eyes. Within a city, there will be many spheres, all overlapping and integrating together to bring the transformation.

Figure 4—Diagram of a Sphere

As the sphere starts to move forward in its function it will attract prayer support from other Christians and it will gather watchmen around it to help signal opportunities or warn of impending dangers. If it is to succeed, it soon becomes a highly organized fighting force, calling down the power of God to fulfill the vision He has given. This is the visionary's part of changing the world about him.

Every Christian has the opportunity to find and fulfill God's vision for him, and although few actually understand all that God is holding out to them, more and more visionaries are starting to catch hold of their vision and run with it. Although within a secular company the sphere will be limited in the natural to performing within the company ethos and ethical structures, it can affect the company in a significant way, often by its success touching the boardroom with significant impact.

As the visionary starts to bring God's plan to bear, the whole company starts to be affected, just as with Arthur Burk. The results will bring prosperity, not only in the financial area, but also in other areas like improved quality of staff, as we saw in Arthur's story, and in the attitudes and atmosphere of that group of people.

Kingdom rule brings Kingdom changes even for those who are not ready to make a commitment to Christ. The more spheres there are in a company, the more quickly it will bring significant change to that company. Even one sphere working on its own can bring significant changes. Across a company where there are several spheres, the company starts to become more Christ like in its heart attitudes and functioning.

Figure 5—Diagram of Secular Company and Figure 6— Diagram of Secular Company With Visionaries Working in It

Figure 5   **Figure 6**

Across the company there are the influences of those who are implementing God's strategies, as shown by the sparkles. Even Christians functioning at a level where they would have had no impact before are having significant impact because of the overall change within the corporate atmosphere.

Whereas the standard corporate men are climbing the corporate ladder in the usual way, grinding their way to the top, looking for significance and acceptance from their senior corporate members, the visionaries working in their spheres are looking only to fulfill their vision.

They are given their significance by God and do not need to look to the corporate management for it. But even though they are not looking for it, they will be given it anyway. They are driven and motivated by God's own hand, not by prestige or money. Their impact is far out of proportion to their size or role because they are implementing God's own plan for that company at that time.

Entrepreneurial Visionaries

There are also those called to a vision outside any currently existing company, worldly or Christian, but who are driven to set up their own structure and run it God's way. Often these are the ones who have an apostolic vision and they will usually find themselves building a workplace church.

Sometimes the visionary may not be a single person, but a team of people. Usually God releases vision to them over a period of time and in stages. God gave Abraham his vision in stages, reinforcing it along the way. God-given vision often does not conform to currently perceived conventional business teaching that is largely predicated on a gospel of lack, but instead it is dependent upon Him to supply in abundance all that is needed to bring forth the fruits and prosper the vision and the company within which it is growing. God Himself sets the boundaries of the vision, incorporating the scope and orientation of operation and identifying functional responsibility. And He expands it when He is ready.

God gives delegated authority to each of the spheres of operation, and puts the responsibility for decision making on the shoulders of those He is anointing for it—the visionary, or visionary team, in the early stages and others as implementation of the vision evolves. God is not into majority management and decision-making, but expects those He is anointing to make decisions. Of course they will listen to wise counsel, but as the leading visionaries, they make the decisions and God holds them accountable for the decisions they make.

The apostolic visionary soon finds God drawing to him others who bring other aspects of the fivefold ministry gifts with them. The pastors, the prophets, teachers, and evangelists will all be drawn by God and knitted to that vision. The model of apostolic fathering starts to increase. Once the fivefold gifts are in place, the building of the Church in some form will automatically follow, as that is the foundation God has laid down.

It is not a coincidence that companies today have divisions that so closely resemble in function and gifting those fivefold ministry gifts God ordained for the building of the Church. Satan counterfeits everything, and he knows how God values His cities and companies. He knows the redemptive gifts and purposes God has revealed for each company and city and nation. Satan knows it; we are the ones who have taken time to wake up to God's strategies. But now is the hour He is awakening us to what He is doing and how He is changing our world to conform to His patterns and plans.

The apostolic fathering role differs from the more traditional caring role we have seen recently in that it does not center on listening to the needy and giving sympathetic responses, which leaves the sheep staying in the same place.

Apostolic fathering on the other hand is focused on bringing freedom and vision to the sheep, as referred to by Jesus in Matthew 11:29, "*take my yoke upon you and learn of Me*." The coach, mentor and father is focused on releasing the sheep into their destiny, the fulfillment of God's purposes for them.

Very soon those whose spheres are functionally complementary to the visionary will find, as the company grows, others gathering around them also, learning from watching them and working alongside them. Fathering also will become a byword of company culture. Their giftings will be multiplied through the demonstration and apprenticing of those who come to them and their gifts and styles will be duplicated and multiplied through on-the-job training.

One important feature of a company built with apostolic vision is the way it functions, not in a hierarchical structure like secular companies and worldly wisdom dictates, but with all visionaries equal and complementary in God's purpose. Since God Himself is providing the resources, there should be no in-company squabbling over the distribution of funding.

Visionaries in every sphere will find they are resourced to the fullness of what they need to fulfill their purpose. They are not being dictated to by the "man at the top" and frustrated by his lack of vision. They are following God's plan with His energy and motivation. In worldly company thinking, it is always difficult to motivate the people further down the ladder, particularly if they cannot see promotion being imminent.

With God's non-hierarchical structure though, all the people are equally motivated since they are driven by His calling. While the apostolic visionary may have the vision for the company, each support visionary that makes up part of that company is separately given motivation by God. Without His vision and motivation to fulfill His calling there, the company would not fulfill its overall purpose. Apostolic visionaries need to remember this when they set the structures of their company.

Soon the city will become aware of this sphere of vision in a corporate vehicle as it moves in to serve the city, as we have seen in Julian's story. New dynamics of fathering will be released into the city and new outreaches to the broken heart of the city will be released. There will be input into the city prayer functions from the company prayer ministries.

The apostolic visionary will find he is soon alongside the other apostles of the area, taking his share in the governmental input into the city governance. The Church will be built and the evangelists will start winning people to the Kingdom in significant numbers. Already we are seeing the early stages of such dreams being realized. There are different ways God uses to transform companies, but it always starts with a man, a vision and prayer.

The Operation of Governments—Interaction and Coordination Between Small Units

Obviously the spheres of operation will overlap to some extent, but within any company there will also be areas that require interaction and coordination, and more specifically, interdependence. These interdependent functioning areas God puts under the responsibility of someone He has gifted for the sphere of operation of government. This function is mentioned only once in the Bible (1 Cor. 12:28) and has the connotation of a pilot steering a ship through difficult and hazardous waters or times.

The purpose of this sphere is to coordinate, administer and steer the sum of the interdependent spheres, never more so than when the interdependent whole is not working and the corporate or company plan laid down by the apostolic and prophetic leaders is heading for difficult waters or to rocks that will sink the plan.

These spheres understand they are to lay down their life to help the other spheres, which we may see in this situation as cogs, to stop them chaffing, grinding and seizing for one spiritual reason or another. I believe visionaries for this sphere are often greatly gifted in the area of discernment.

This sphere manages the interdependence of all the other spheres after the apostolic and prophetic plan is agreed on and passed to the corporate organization to move ahead. The efficiency of the functioning of the operation of governments can make or break a company in the same way each of the spheres can make or break that department's contribution, and with it the effectiveness of the company to which it belongs.

As each part of the company responds to implementing God's vision in its particular area so transformation begins and changes start to happen in its own sphere, and the company as a whole changes, depending on the quantity of spheres working out God's visions within it.

The spheres are still affected by the overall culture of the company however, and unless the overall climate of the company can be changed and brought in line with what God wants to achieve, its growth can be limited as a result. The spheres may come to the view they need some help with the change management required, and there is well-proven change management practice that can be usefully employed.

Overnight Miracles?

Can a company be changed overnight? Even from the top level, I don't believe so. There are certain key elements we have to take into account. God shows us His character in the Bible through storytelling about patterns of behavior. In the same way, God changes organizations through transforming patterns of behavior based on His principles. The result is that the organization begins to reflect Christ to a greater degree. The continued transformation of that organization then becomes a change management task.

Transformation Management

The science of transformation is well established, but it is interesting to look at it in the light of transformation of corporations remembering that it also applies in principle to cities. Taking it to its simplest, the internal environment of an organization can be regarded as falling into two types of environment: causal and expressed.

In the causal environment we have structure and process. These directly affect the culture and climate we see expressed in the daily life of its staff, their attitudes and behavior to one another, and to the clients and suppliers.

Figure 7—Diagram of Analytical Model of Structures and Processes of a Company

Analytical Model of Structure and Process

STRUCTURE AND PROCESS			
ROLES	CONFIGURATION	TECHNOLOGY	PLANNING & CONTROL SYSTEMS
INFORMATION	DECISION MAKING	HR POLICY	COMMUNICATIONS
CONFLICT RESOLUTION	INTER-UNIT COOPERATION (INTEGRATION)	INTEGRATION	

CULTURE AND CLIMATE

BEHAVIOUR IN ORGANISATIONS

From Organisational Analysis, Ron Drew Associates

The structures and processes of the company include all those things that internally affect the behavior of its staff, such as personnel programs, technologies, innovations, planning and control systems, integration and so on.

The degree to which the structure and processes of a company can be changed, is the degree to which you can affect the culture and climate of that company. You can't touch culture and climate directly because they are the cumulative result of what happens when structures and processes are applied to the workforce. It is their collective manifest behavior.

What we have to do to transform an organization in order to bring a greater reflection of Christ is to change the ideology element of culture and climate. We write the ideology of the organization based on righteousness and drawn from biblical principles.

Figure 8—Diagram of Analytical Model of Culture and Climate of a Company

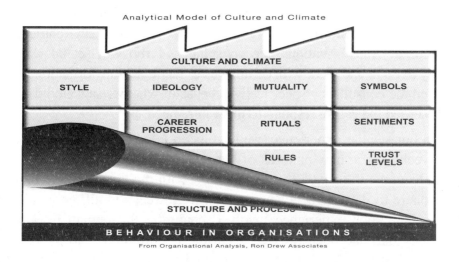

Analytical Model of Culture and Climate

CULTURE AND CLIMATE

| STYLE | IDEOLOGY | MUTUALITY | SYMBOLS |

| | CAREER PROGRESSION | RITUALS | SENTIMENTS |

| | | RULES | TRUST LEVELS |

STRUCTURE AND PROCESS

BEHAVIOUR IN ORGANISATIONS

From Organisational Analysis, Ron Drew Associates

The culture and climate of an organization is the representation of the behavior found in the organization measured across a number of headings. If the passage of promotion is by having sex with the managing director, or a group of directors, that opens the doorway to a sexual spirit that begins to be rewarded and enshrined in the career progression element of culture and climate. The people within the company are shaped by the behavior of their peers and sexual activity expressed in a career progression is reinforced.

People can leave or they can choose not to be advanced that way, but they will not change the climate within the organization once it has been established unless the structure and process is changed. If a culture rewards greed, you can expect that organization to be filled with a spirit of greed; if it reinforces backstabbing, you will find a political spirit, and so on. This is well understood by organizational behavior theory.

It is important to be aware of the prevailing culture of the company when we're considering spirits in the organization. We need to put gatekeepers in place to take Kingdom authority in the name of Jesus over demonic spirits if we are serious about achieving God's plans and purposes through a corporate entity.

Corporate Transformations

I believe we are going to have whole consultancies like Diamond Thinking run by Steve and Lydia Mallison-Jones and Cognitive Learning run by Jerome and Machelle Joseph that are going to go in and help people transform their companies into Kingdom environments. Corporate Transformations, the consultancy I run will set up teams ready to go in and work with companies to facilitate transformation. We started the consultancy specifically because of what we saw God doing and sensed the call to respond to this future need.

In our secular experience, we have been into organizations and in 13 weeks put in new patterns of behavior based on these principles. We then take the next 13 weeks to work with the client to help them to adhere to these new behaviors. That's 26 weeks in all, only half a year. One such experience involved changing the human resource strategy that had been focused on hiring people motivated by greed and self-advancement to those motivated and rewarded by team and corporate advancement. This improved customer loyalty, cleansed the organizations of fox type behaviors, and improved profitability.

In classic organization theory and without transformation management it used to take 10 to 15 years to happen by evolution. The problem of course is that we are human and keep returning to our default settings. We like what we hear and we say we're going to do it, but a few weeks later we're back in the old routine and at square one again. That's what the second period of 13 weeks is about—keeping it going and establishing the habits that bring transformation.

City Transformation—How Does it Work?

Citywide transformation is following the hand of God and working with Him to bring coordinated city change. In essence it is the same as transformation in an organization. What we have to do to transform a city in order to bring a greater reflection of Christ is to influence all the elements of a functioning city such as local government, business, education, retail, manufacturing, corporate offices, the police and the national health service—in short all the city structures that bring management and control of wealth and influence across a city.

Each one is now a sphere of the city. It is the unseen realm of powers, principalities, rulers, etc., that control the collective behavior of the population of the city that has given the legal right to those powers and principalities over generations. This collective behavior of the city is really the prevailing ideology that is the guiding element of culture and climate in transformation management.

Think of Brighton, England or San Francisco in the USA, where the collective population has given legal right to homosexuals, lesbian lifestyles and high abortion rates, and has made those cities famous for acceptance of those behaviors. In Brighton it had reached the point of more than 20% of the local council being homosexual or lesbian, and that city structure enshrined an ideology that is the opposite of a reflection of Christ. Also the number of aborted babies reached a level that was greater than those being born!

To show how far this has gone, a national paper in the U.K. published research proposals for city rejuvenation and growth stating that cities would die if they do not support the approval of homosexual and lesbian lifestyles. For example, Sunderland was quoted as being dead and Manchester as being ready for growth.

There are different spiritual authorities and levels given by God for unlocking the population of a city from the powers, principalities, etc. These have been given to the apostolic and prophetic leaders of the structures with management control of wealth and influence across the city. They assemble at apostolic and prophetic councils to the city. Watchmen, intercessors and the local church all have a part to play in releasing the population who work in those structures and live in the territory.

Figure 9—Apostolic Council and Its Interacting Spheres in a City

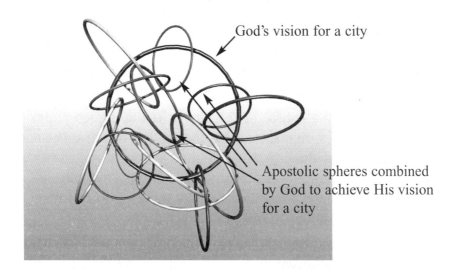

God's vision for a city

Apostolic spheres combined by God to achieve His vision for a city

Just as a company has links with others, including suppliers and clients for example, so cities will have spiritual links with other cities and towns or regions. These will need to be identified and put in place. Often these links will transcend national boundaries, and links across nations will need to be set up.

Just as individual spheres will have people committed to pray for them and for God's purposes to be fulfilled in and through them, so cities will have intercessors and watchmen working in every element of a city sphere to bring God's purposes to pass in that territory.

Just as there are significant linkages between spheres in any company, so there are spiritually significant links to be discovered between cities and regions in any nation. Just as there is a need for communication and the dissemination of information within and between company spheres, so in the spheres of the city there is the need for communication and information to be disseminated.

Cities are larger than companies and the difficulties of maintaining full communications can be challenging, but answers can and must be found; for where God opens a need, He Himself ensures the supply of all that is required to meet that need.

So we see God networking people together across regions and nations to affect change of the whole. I believe that every city and every nation has a precise definable purpose and vision that God has given it. And the combination of all the corporate spheres and even smaller spheres come together to create and fulfill that. God has been training up His dedicated communications professionals to be able to design the communication interdependence across a city.

One such person is Suzie Hamlin from Leeds, U.K., whose story you can read in the next chapter. Another dedicated communications specialist I am working with is Ron from Fusionpage, Texas in the USA. They have satisfied customers in 75 countries worldwide. People like these are being raised up to cope with the rising need for communications across cities and nations.

Cities and Spheres

God gives a man a sphere of authority to help transform a city, just as in company transformation. To the extent that man is walking with the Lord and has responded to His refining and character development, God then activates that sphere in terms of energizing the man, motivating him and giving him vision that will bring to pass the fulfillment of God's plans and purposes for that sphere of the city. The sphere becomes that man's field, his given territory to rule over and transform for the Lord, as in Genesis 1:28.

The man may be working away in his sphere, completely unaware of God's plans for the whole city, but at some time the Lord then gets him involved with, and gives him the opportunity to sow into, His vision, plans and purposes for the bigger picture, be it citywide, nationwide or worldwide. While he may not be one of God's city-level visionaries, he will still have the opportunity to play his part in the citywide transformation through regular contact with other people and communicating information about God's work in his sphere.

A City Taker's Story

Being a city taker is not what most people think. This is the story of one man being groomed by God to impact his city with apostolic vision. He's also called to impact his nation and other nations. He's building the Church in his workplace. He's not running a conventional business, he's not a conventional apostle, nor is he building conventional church. But he's one of God's men for this hour and this is a brief summary of his story.

Richard Nicol came out of a standard suburban home in outer London, the middle of three brothers. Bright, intelligent and a "gad about lad," he was always popular with the "blokes" and always in the "pub." Married to Karen when he was still young, he took a while to grow up and find his feet. Karen came from a broken home and an abusive childhood, but together they made a good team.

Mr. Nicol started work in NatWest and gained a lot of experience in personnel and finance management. He moved around the banking environment, making contacts and developing his career before ending up in Birmingham.

Being a natural entrepreneur, he decided to set up on his own. Gamekeeper turned poacher, he was organizing finance, writing business plans and brokering property deals. He started in the spare room at home, doing the plans and organizing money for a wide range of developers and investors. He already had involvement in a couple of golf courses, organizing finance and business plans for them, and planned to put together a company specifically to focus on golf course consultancy and finance. One of his property clients asked him to arrange some finance for a hotel project in the center of Birmingham—a crazy idea for an old doss house.

It was the start of a long relationship. Mr. Nicol wrote the business plan and organized some money for them. But eight days after they opened the business, they fired the general manager. Mr. Nicol had just introduced them to an important banking relationship and being concerned that the £3 million they had been lent wasn't going to be repaid, he rushed over to help with managing the hotel and stayed six years.

God had thrust him into the hotel business out of nowhere. His only credential for being in the hotel business was that he used to be a guest, but now he was suddenly running a 250-bed hotel in the middle of Birmingham that was teetering on the brink of falling over before it had even gotten started. It was a tremendous learning curve, but he thrived on it. The business became very successful. He employed 170 people and made it happen. When God has you on the fast track, everything comes together at once.

Opening His Eyes

Then God started teaching him about life. "Business in the Community" made an approach to the hotel to take the managers on a tour around Borstal Heath, a very deprived area around the inner city. It was a seeing-is-believing tour and it made a believer out of him.

There were people living in the inner city a mile and a half from his desk but he had never been there. It was a trigger time when God placed compassion in his heart. There were other encounters too, including a sink school for excluded kids. The job did not make any sense, but they were getting results, as the kids were getting qualifications. They were doing things other schools would not even contemplate.

Mr. Nicol ended up as chair of governors. Eighty-one percent of children had English as a second language. Sixty-one percent had free school meals. A cocktail of Muslim, Afro-Caribbean, English and Yemeni kids gave him a real window on the community.

Mr. Nicol found himself doing a job that he had no experience for and no credentials for, but it was what he was best at. He knew it is what he was made for. Soon he was in a 450-bed hotel in the middle of a prime site in Birmingham.

He appointed a Christian as his personnel manager and developed a policy of being specific about where he would recruit people. The employment service, the job centers and the employment resource centers were not targeting the poorer areas of Birmingham, so he went into the middle of the community and put a tent in their carnival as a jobs fair. It won the carnival award and soon 10% of his staff were long-term unemployed people. They started to see their potential released under Richard's gift of fathering, and they became loyal, flexible and purposeful people.

Challenged and Refined

Mr. Nicol and his wife Karen had moved to an evangelical church where there was a school for expository preaching. New windows opened for him as he learned to preach and hear God speak through the Bible. He found guiding scriptures for his life, such as 1 Corinthians 13 on love, Ephesians 5:25, on loving your wife as Christ loved the church and Matthew 6:24, on not serving both God and mammon.

Mr. Nicol felt God challenge him. He was earning £150,000 a year but some of the business practices he was expected to do were at odds with what he thought and believed and felt. He knew God was facing him up with a choice. Do you believe what it says in the Bible or not? And are you going to be obedient to it or not?

Mr. Nicol left his job without any money, severance pay or anywhere to go. One of his contacts asked him to make an offer for a 37-acre site in Birmingham. It had a golf driving range at one end, with a woodland, an archaeological site and a school adjoining it. Mr. Nicol knew God had to have put the deal together. The owners had spent almost two million developing the site but they accepted his offer and an exchange of contracts to purchase the site for £825,000 even with a tiny deposit of £2,500. Only God can do such a deal!

For nine months while he negotiated the purchase of the site, God put him through that refining process that people go through before God can really trust them with something that is going to glorify Him. It was a nightmare time for Mr. Nicol and his wife, as their marriage was being shaken and they were both hurting.

They had no income, their overdraft was up to the limit, every credit card was up to the limit and they had had to put their house on the market. They did not know what was happening to them. The final crunch came when three weeks short of the deadline for buying the site, Mr. Nicol's bank contact announced he was leaving the company and pulled out of the site deal. Mr. Nicol was shocked, as he had a contract on the site and was to close on it in three weeks.

Then God stepped in. The first of the week, another guy came from the bank, read the business plan, thought it was good and agreed to it. It was the run up to Christmas, but 14 days short of the completion date, he got confirmation the banking facilities were through. At the same time his other investors came on board and the purchase was completed. It was as if God just stretched them all the way there.

Over the nine months while his marriage was being grounded in God, the environmental reports for the site came through—clean as a whistle. The planning application went forward for 132 bedrooms, a conference center and a health and fitness club with a pool and a gym, together with a 95-place preschool nursery and 5,000 square feet of offices.

Mr. Nicol went to the planning committee meeting and watched other prestige applications being refused or asked for further information. It was tense because he wanted to operate in the wrong part of town, outside the guidelines, and was asking for something that was unique.

The chairman of the planning committee said, "Host center, recommended for approval." He looked around at everybody and stamped it "Approved," without a word of disagreement. With the benefit of that planning consent, the site that Mr. Nicol had paid £825,000 for is now valued at £3.275 million.

Mr. Nicol and his wife went away to the Maldives and fell in love again, starting the healing in their relationship, for which God had laid the foundations. It was as if He was saying, "Get your act together. The Kingdom principles are: don't worry about the money, make sure your house is in order, love Me with all your heart and love your wife like Christ loves the church." What Richard and Karen Nicol can now see is that the gifts that He has given them go together. Karen is an intercessor, a watchman and a warrior. And Mr. Nicol is a builder, a planter, and he is out there in the front line doing God's new stuff.

Catching His Vision

God spoke to him powerfully about his business, planting a passion and vision in him that still brings tears to his eyes. The vision for Host is to create an environment where the people who are working there are modeling, coaching, mentoring and equipping people in what it takes to be a host, to provide warm and generous behavior to strangers and guests and to do it in a social and business capacity.

This vision was born from the hotelier in the story of the Good Samaritan. He is the one Christ trusts with broken people. His responsibility is to provide them hospitality. So Mr. Nicol is turning his site into an environment where he can train people to provide hospitality as a gateway to employment.

About Host, Mr. Nicol says: "There are 47,000 people in the city without a job and 20,000 to 25,000 jobs in the city. But the kids that haven't got a job, they haven't got the skills. And they haven't got the skills because they haven't got the family structures. And they haven't got the mums and the dads. They haven't got the role models and they haven't had the experiences I've had, they've had the experiences Karen's had. They've been abused.

"So all we want to do is to create an environment where the people who are working there are modeling, coaching, mentoring and equipping people in what it takes to be a host, to provide warm and generous behavior to strangers and guests and to do it in a social and business capacity.

"A lot of those things are things that we should be picking up in the family, picking up from our mums and our dads. But if you haven't got one, you can't. If you eat in McDonald's, you don't know how to lay a table, if you sleep in a sleeping bag in the corner, you don't know how to make a bed, and if you live in tennis shoes, you probably don't know what a shoe brush is for. When people stay in hotels they have a level of expectation that makes you feel a fool if you can't meet it.

"The colleges and training schools do their part, but actually we are in that practical area of saying, 'Knock, knock, knock, come on, get out of bed. Alarm clock, uniform, minibus, shoes. Have you had any breakfast? Can you read? What do you want to do? What are the issues for your home?'

"As an employer, we are showing the love of Jesus. The vision for the company is that 60% percent of the staff would be people that they would employ. They would not necessarily have to be Christians, but they are going to have to behave like Christians. The kids, the career changers and the people who've retired and their pensions don't meet the bills any more, can come back into this environment and be equipped to work in Birmingham's new industry of hospitality. We are making Host the hallmark of hospitality. It's not a logo, or an icon to look at; it's a badge that they wear, skills they take out into life."

Prayer

Mr. Nicol prays with a group of fellow businessmen regularly. He understands the importance of fellowship for Christians in the marketplace. They meet and talk about the issues of being in business, including not only the work they have to do, but also the people they have to work with, their wives' reaction to what is going on at work and the many other challenges there are, such as cash flow. Every Monday morning they e-mail each other and share what's been going on and they all meet once a month for breakfast and fellowship. Recently they have started other cells across the city and nation.

Mr. Nicol also prays in the office and with fellow Christians in the company. They also have meetings where other Christians come, and he has extensive prayer cover from home. Mrs. Nicol meets every week with a group and they pray for the company in a big way.

"Work and prayer opens a door on Monday morning that used to get shut on Sunday night. There's more about church for me now on the other six days a week than there is on a Sunday. I work mainly with non-Christians, but God turns up and impacts people's lives there.

"I've been involved in the finance group of the church. I've led groups of kids in church. But there's something about local church that just doesn't touch it. I can only speak as a bloke; it's probably even more challenging for ladies in business. We can help move chairs and we can go to a conference once a year with a load of blokes. But actually the gifts are to expand and mature the church and take the church out to the people; it's not about the guy who stands in the pulpit.

"That's not the shape of church I read about in the Bible. That's not who Jesus picked. He went out into the marketplace and he picked 12 blokes. And he sent them out in ones and twos and they turned the world upside down. That's what it's about: being the ones Jesus can trust with the people."

Sooner or later the city will invite Mr. Nicol to be part of their apostolic council—when there is one. He will be inputting into his city just as Julian does in Guildford. He will be able to communicate with others of like mind and calling in his city. They will be following the hand of God, sharing information and working together to coordinate what they see God doing. Current jargon denotes such gatherings for hearing God, prayer and God's strategy planning as "war rooms."

War Rooms

God showed me how a war room can coordinate the prayer efforts of the whole city. Then He showed me how the city generals and ministries are scattered across the city as a series of territories, like the spheres within a company. The spheres may be tangible areas of territory like city geographies, or they may be conceptual areas of territory like people groupings such as the elderly, the media, etc.

Through releasing His motivation, energy, resources, plans and purposes, God leads and coordinates these spheres across a city and He does so in exactly the same way He leads, coordinates and transforms an organization or a company.

The obvious problem of course, is that for this strategy to work fully, God's men need to bring transformation to all the elements that make up the structures of a city but which are currently keeping the existing inhabitants bound under enemy powers and principalities.

The apostolic generals' war room may be the core generator of the coordinated strategy for the city and a center for intercessors and watchmen, but unless the people who meet there are functioning across the city and interacting within and through their own different spheres of activity, they will have nothing vital and new to contribute to the city-reaching strategy. Obviously it would not be realistic to expect the generals to come only from one area of expertise or geography.

Prayers Arise

Prayer is the engine of the war room strategy. Across cities and nations God is releasing His call to those who are gifted with stamina in prayer, or gifted with revelatory vision as watchmen. Now is the time for these men and women of God to arise and stand to take their place as valued members of the Body.

Much of it has already been happening, as 24-hour prayer has been rising up seven days a week in many areas. But this is still only the beginning. God is networking even those of us who feel we have little time to pray for our nations into groups to watch and pray for our nations or other nations as we feel He is leading us. These are truly amazing times.

God Hears Every Word Spoken to Him in Prayer

The call to prayer is loud and strong and no one can say they cannot do it. Together we can impact nations, we can impact cities, and we can change situations. Together we can watch and pray and make the difference. Even half an hour a day can make a difference.

City watches are being set up in most cities these days and the cry of God resounds around us—come and pray, come and watch, come and release the purposes of God for your city. Come people, come and pray, come and watch, for now is the hour when all is to be released from heaven, and the nations of the world will stand in awe at what the hand of the Lord does.

Redemptive Gift—The Riches Within Our Field

Most of us make ourselves the center of the universe. But really, everything we do is in the context of God's plans and purposes for the world, then continents, then nations, then cities, then parts of cities, then corporate entities, then individual families or individuals.

This is necessary because God ties vision to the redemptive gift, the purposes that He gave for the land. We can't really appreciate contextually what God is doing until we can understand His redemptive gift for our place of influence.

All that takes place in a territory is seen in God's eyes through His purposes for the land according to the varied redemptive gifts that He has placed in every different area of land. To gain deeper insight into what God is doing so we can work with Him more fully, we have to know what the redemptive gift on our particular sector of land is.

We find this out through the work of spiritual and secular historians and through revelation. All our understanding of, and expectation of, that territory has to be filtered through God's fulfilling of the redemptive gift upon that land.

As we harness the redemptive gift of our land, we find a new level of power available to us. This is when we see God upholding His plans through His power. Unless we mine this resource we are functioning with the equivalent of one hand tied behind our backs.

We also have to take into account what season we are in, in relation to God's timing. The Bible uses the word *chronos* for general time, but then there is *kairos* time, the time set for a spiritual breakthrough. God was talking to me about this through Ecclesiastes 3, where it speaks of "*a time to reap and a time to sow.*"

God is always in the process of working out His purposes, whatever time we are in. We fall under God's timing for all things. We may be in a time of closeness with Him, a time for embracing. We may be in times of warfare or times of peace.

Figure 10—Diagram of Ecclesiastes 3

Not only are we subject to God's timing for us as individuals, but we also fall subject to God's timing for the section of population we are in, such as the city or our particular territory or field of function. We see in Judges how the nation of Israel was swinging between times of oppression, to get them to turn back to Him, and times of deliverance.

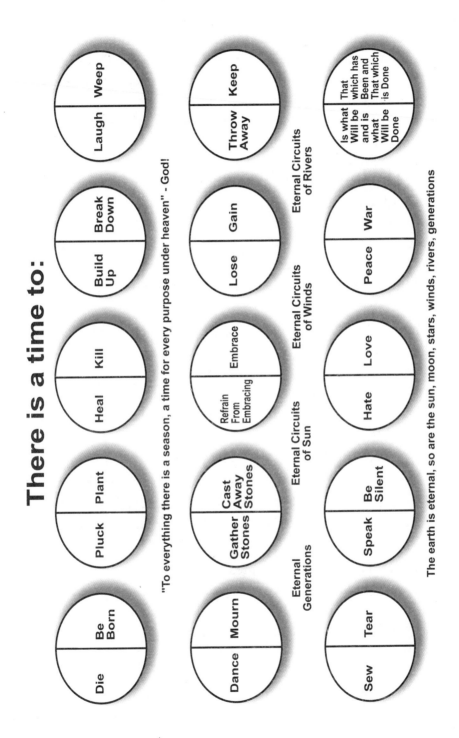

Figure 10 - Diagram of Ecclesiastes 3

It is the same today: we come into times of oppressions and times of deliverance in our cities accordingly, as God works to get the city or nation to turn back to His plans and purposes for them. There is a tendency to think that under the judges Israel spent most of her time being oppressed as God sought to draw her back in repentance to Him, but in fact, as the diagram clearly shows, there were many more years spent in deliverance than in oppression.

Figure 11—Diagram of Times of Oppression and Deliverance

The point we have reached in each of these timing scales will affect what we are going through, our emotions, our physical environment and our progress. Where our friends are will affect them and our interaction. Where our territory is will affect us and our progress, as well as where our nation is in God's timing and God's purposes.

It may not be a "kairos" time for a breakthrough, but nevertheless the Lord is working out an Ecclesiastes type of circle in each of our lives. There are 30 seasons mentioned in Ecclesiastes to take into account and I see them like control dials of a plane. So to find out where we are and where the city is, we should first be looking to line up the dials with where God is.

Is He trying to bring the people back by allowing some oppression, or have they recognized their sin and are on their way back after He is done delivering them? These different scenarios also look different according to the redemptive gift for that particular area of land.

Once we have that as the context, we can grasp a wider picture of where we are. We know God is motivating each of our spheres according to 1 Corinthians 12:6-7. Therefore He must be motivating each of us in the context of His redemptive gift upon the land, and according to what stage of being oppressed or delivered the people or corporate organizations are, and whether it's a "kairos" moment. In a "kairos" time of breakthrough, everything just happens and it all looks very simple, but most of us probably toil with the Lord for quite a few years before our "kairos" time comes.

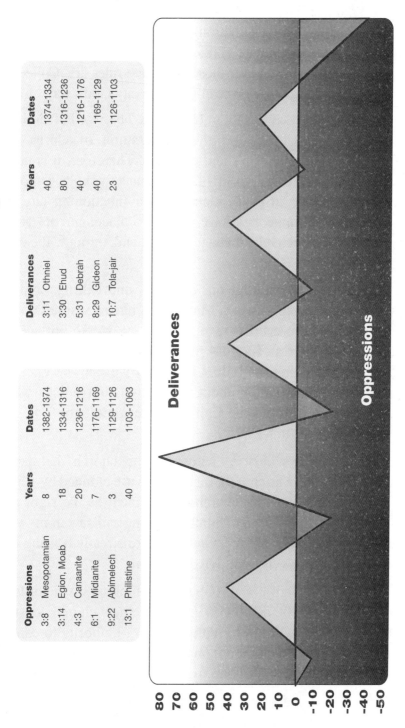

Figure 11 - Diagram of Times of Oppression and Deliverance

Impacting Cities

God impacts His city through corporate entities that He has envisioned, those corporate entities take land, they become landlords, and they govern by whatever those corporate rules are. Collectively all those corporate organizations can govern a city God's way.

I know that is open to a lot of challenge. The Word of God says that He builds His Church on the cornerstone of Christ and the foundations of His apostles and prophets. Therefore, it is now being accepted all around the world—that God has workplace apostles and prophets that take in every element of a functioning city. We can begin to see that once they have risen into place, and are envisioned by God, He collectively manages them, and through them He can transform a city.

Most of us are walking out our gifts and callings and being a witness in our place of work. Many of us have a vision to see Christ come and act powerfully in our place of work, but we are not gathering together as fivefold ministries and building the Church. We may be winning souls to Christ and we may be changing the hearts of our workmates about the gospel, but unless we have a specific vision to build the Church, we are unlikely to be building an **apostolic vision**.

It is not always easy to recognize the church that people are building these days as church, for our eyes are clouded by generations of accepting the existing church environment as the right one. Nor can we readily identify any church behaving as I saw in my visions in Sunderland. Yet, they are there and they are already bearing the fruits of their faithfulness like Mr. Nicol's vision.

We need to be building the Church the biblical way in order to take cities. We need to be helping to grow these new church constructs, as without them we will not have the power or authority to confront the prince of the air in his seat of control over cities, tear down his works, and wrest his throne from him in Jesus' mighty name.

Only God can do this, the works of man alone cannot. God has been talking to us for several years now, through his prophets and

Bible teachers worldwide, about how He is bringing a new church construct into being. He has declared loud and clear that now is the time for Him to bring increase to His Body so that we are ready to confront satan in these last days, for the battle is looming.

I see God tackling the cities and changing the face of organizations that are being run on worldly principles. The fact is that most current morality has moved from the biblical principles of right and wrong to embrace an alternative view that believes there are no absolutes, only shades of perspective.

Only belief in a God of absolute truth and absolute love can allow concepts of absolute right and wrong in business terms. Only a God of love can justify the outworking of business finances to care for the underprivileged, not as a tax dodge or for publicity, but from a heart overflowing with God's love.

Satan's forces are at work and holding the people of the cities captive to him wherever he is able to function. But God is moving His armies into place and satan's time is running out. Jesus defeated our enemy at the Cross, but He waits now for us to implement that victory by using our authority to tear down satan's works and free our cities from his oppression.

Everywhere we look, we can see satan holding people captive, in every workplace, in every residential complex, in the government, in law enforcement and in businesses. The time is coming to overturn that control and release the authority of our Lord into those areas.

To get the corporate entity working how God wants it, we have to go back to the biblical model where the cornerstone is Christ, upon whom stand the apostles and prophets. God then brings fivefold ministry to that corporation, for He has said,

And He Himself gave some to be apostles, some prophets, some evangelists, and some pastors and teachers, for the equipping of the saints for the work of ministry, for the edifying of the body of Christ... (Ephesians 4:11-12 NKJV).

The people in the organizations that are being transformed, whose collective behavior transforms a city, need the fivefold ministry to be working in those corporations. Then we will see the dynamic of people being born again, going on discipleship programs and being equipped for the work of the corporate organization envisioned by God.

At this point we begin to get significant transformation within the organizations, and that collectively brings transformation across the city. People, Christian and non-Christian, will be talking about the visible changes happening in the city. Most will be welcoming what's happening. The heart-cry of God for ministry to the underprivileged will be poured out across the city and change will be happening on every front as companies and conglomerates start to take hold of God's heart in outreach to the needs they see across the city.

Councils and police will see significant change being wrought citywide and a lightness will start to filter into everyone's awareness. City change is not a dream; it's a reality. It's the heart of God for our times and we shall see it.

How fast this change happens simply depends on us. Whether we grasp hold of the challenge with both hands and run with God into our future, or we stick to the comfortable and ordinary that we know and play it safe, it is up to us.

CHAPTER 4

Facilitating Citywide Vision

Communication is the lifeblood of unity, whether it be in a family, a company or across a city or nation. The success of any unit is always related to the functional competence of its communications systems. Contracts are missed and wars won by the level of information available. Communication facilitates a Kingdom building, Body mindset as opposed to the divisive ivory tower mindsets that have been prevalent in the past, and have been so restrictive to cross-city mission.

Good communication can show people what resources are available, help to avoid unnecessary duplication, and enable the Church in the city to fulfill its thrust to inhabit and establish dominion across every area of the territory. Hope and mercy missions are similarly facilitated, both by highlighting areas that have been forgotten and by galvanizing workplace organizations and structures to release wealth from their increases into specific areas of need.

Communication breaks down isolation and brings people together across geographies and cultural divides in shared vision and encouragement. It helps to serve the Ephesians 4:12 call to the ministry gifts in the Body:

> *...for the equipping of the saints for the work of ministry, for the edifying of the body of Christ...* (NKJV).

Communications Hub

Even within a small organization or church, communication is the hub of successful management and maintaining good relations between people, and in making people feel valued. We are created as social beings and communications is at the core of all our social structures.

Unfortunately, all too often our communications systems are flawed. When it comes to citywide communications, the difficulties are multiplied many times over, yet are even more essential than in smaller people groupings, as communication is our main form of relationship. Misunderstandings occur frequently at all levels of relationship, and if we are to build citywide relationships for the gospel's sake, we need to have those communications channels in place, functioning well and accessible to all.

Among the new things God has birthed in recent years is the communications revolution. It is no accident that it comes at this time, when God is preparing to pour out His Spirit in power upon all of His children. The "day of the saints," when all believers will walk in His power for miracles, is coming upon us fast, and we need to have access to information about all that God is doing so that we can keep track of where He is going.

Just like Jesus, we need to follow our Father's example and do as He is doing. Communications is providing a resource to enable an increased understanding of what God is doing in our cities and of the times and seasons of God's purposes in which we are living. We have to know that God is the center of our city, and it's His plans and purposes that count. When we get ourselves and our organizations out of thinking we are at the center, we can begin to look for our membership ministry to what He is doing.

Digital Neighborhoods Facilitate Change

Information is the new currency of this age and as the Body of Christ seeks to come together across territories to prepare for the new move God has promised, grassroots communications has started to take on a new level of importance for today's citywide Church.

Electronic communications are undoubtedly a convenience over the telephone and face-to-face meetings, and although they lack that physical contact so necessary for real relationship, God has made the technology available to us at this time and most people are keen to exploit it to the maximum.

In recent years, communication has opened up to Christians across territories and nations through the electronic media. Web sites are very common among churches and ministries. The advancement of a simple site to an interactive digital neighborhood is a small step and one that many have already found extremely helpful. Digital neighborhoods are relationally based Internet applications that connect to community, and respond collectively to the needs of those who partake in them.

Easier than sending e-mail, this global village opens the communications doorway, bringing a new dimension of speed to current communications between Christians across cities and nations. As Walter Wilson wrote in the *Internet Church*, "What if God were to give the Church a global communications tool capable of reaching the entire world?... He already has." One such communications tool is the WorkplaceMinisters.com digital neighborhood.

Communications Excellence

When God looks at a city, He sees the Church in the city, He doesn't regard all the different denominations or expressions of church as being different bodies, they are all part of His one Body. It is necessary then to bring about an interchange of communications between all the different representations of that Body across a city.

These will be traditional denominational churches, including the newer charismatic local churches, but they will also include the workplace churches, incubator churches, children's churches and other expressions of the Body we are starting to see breaking forth across the cities.

Enabling ongoing multi-way communication facilitates the breaking down of barriers that currently exist horizontally across cities and vertically in Church—defined by Dr. Bill Hamon as "the one, universal, many-membered, corporate Body of Christ."

Leaders currently cannot help but be bottlenecks to communications vertically in their own organizations and horizontally to all other membership ministries to the Body across the city. Currently God is raising many of His people across nations who are envisioned to facilitate communications needs across cities and national boundaries to bring unity to the Body of Christ and prepare them to break out into the fullness of what God has for their city or nation.

Just as one of God's strategies is to enable a flow of communications across boundaries, so it is satan's strategy to confuse and bring ineffective communications. We all know the problems that can be wrought by ineffective, chaotic communications, and we see it happening again and again in the Body of Christ as satan confounds man's strategies with his tricks. But satan cannot confound God.

People Come First

Digital communications has gotten bad press in some areas, but contrary to how it has been portrayed, people and their needs are at the center of all good communications. The Internet and digital mobile phones are now a daily part of life for many, but there are still some, particularly in areas of global isolation or social deprivation, where such technology is as yet unavailable, or ineffective.

The purpose of communications across a city is to be inclusive of all, not only for those with access to computers. Any citywide system therefore has to make provision for those unable to receive data electronically. Any nationwide or global system also has to be able to accommodate such people, or the system is not doing its job. Sharing information can bring significant benefits to all, so all must be accommodated.

Speeding Up the Talk

Using modern technology speeds up communication and helps individuals overcome existing constraints and limitations. Previous methods of communication were heavily reliant on existing church relationships, and on telephone and face-to-face meetings.

Within a small territory that can be difficult, especially if the people concerned are fitting meetings into busy schedules. But when it comes to wider or even international communications, the problems significantly increase. By comparison, in a digital neighborhood people can connect however they want, whenever they want.

Kingdom advice centers, local churches, workplace churches, watchmen with prophetic words, all are fulfilling God's call for relationship and pointing toward the redemptive gift in their territories. God gets back into our communications through digital neighborhoods like Workplace Ministers digital neighborhood because we instantly put Him back in that place where He is giving unction to people around the clock. He energizes, motivates, contacts, and divinely links people by His unction and it can be anywhere, anytime, across the city or the globe.

In seeking to establish an electronic citywide communications system, one of the problems is that not everyone is yet in place, nor will they be. God is bringing people to maturity and fulfillment at different times, and His apostles and visionaries of this hour are all at different stages of release.

Often no one is coordinating the work across cities, particularly since some of it may be done in other cities or nations. No one human being can orchestrate this coordination. This is reserved for Jesus, working through the Holy Spirit, the only one who can be everywhere at once, with the intellect, purity of thought and infinite wisdom to coordinate the Body.

God's apostles may not even know who they are; they may need to be drawn forward. Workplace apostles may be getting ready to step forward at different times. Local church apostles may be ready at different times to move into the fullness of transforming their city. In a digital neighborhood all can post their work, and emerging apostles and visionaries can be recognized by others. There will be a natural distillation as people find their places in the cross-city vision.

In practical terms, what happens is that each visionary's sphere can come out as a Web page within a digital neighborhood, and they can articulate there how God energizes, motivates, resources, and gives them plans and purposes. Others in the digital neighborhood can see what stage they have reached by reading what they are doing and discussing it with them.

God can connect people whenever He wants via the digital neighborhood in ways that could be lengthy and tortuous through currently existing channels. Connections can be made when they are needed, and time saved by eliminating unnecessary duplication. Digital neighborhoods encourage relationship through written media, but are much more relationally centered than simply sending e-mails back and forth.

The previously mentioned challenge of finding out who the apostles are, for example, is reduced because as they contribute their input to the city digital neighborhood, they will become apparent by their fruits and by the witness God puts in the Body corporate for that city. God can therefore interact between people, drawing out relationships quickly and easily and bonding hearts.

He can also make available all current knowledge about the city: the spiritual mapping, the intercessory prayers, the watchmen's report, the priestly apostles' advice, the workplace apostles' input and so on. All the information is transferred to knowledge management format so it becomes accessible to the whole Body of Christ.

Any member of the Body of Christ can go onto the digital neighborhood pages and see what God has already revealed to people about that area. For example, on the St. Albans, England digital neighborhood public areas, the spiritual mapping team has a Web site showing the work they've done in St. Albans. This sort of information file could be available for intercessors in the area to use for prayer.

Protection Versus Control

It is impossible to protect people from all things, especially from our enemy who prowls around like a devouring lion to see whom he can destroy. Unfortunately traditional protective processes have also led to a locking-up to one degree or another. In the past, local church leaders held themselves responsible for protecting their sheep, but in these final days, the Word of God tells us there will be false teachers, false prophets, false miracles workers and wolves among us, and that even the elect will be in some part be deceived.

It is clear therefore that God is allowing these things to happen, so He must be expecting us to be able to resist such things, to know and hang on to His truth through it all. To do that we must all stay personally close to Him and let Him heighten our discernment.

Anyone who has raised children knows the difficulty of releasing them into their adult freedom and all the dangers that go with it, but unless they are given their freedom, their maturity and development is limited. So it is with Christians. Once we reach a level of maturity, God expects us to make our own decisions and be responsible for them. We have to let go of our milk diet, accept solid food, and discern between good and evil, as described in Hebrews 5:14.

No longer can we rely on and trust others to tell us what is and is not acceptable to God. We must stay close to Him and weigh for ourselves, by the standard of His truth, what is acceptable to Him, and rely on His Holy Spirit to guide our hearts and minds so that we are not deceived.

It is the same principal in digital neighborhoods and with all Web sites. The tenet of "buyer beware" holds true. We are responsible for weighing and discerning what is truth and from God for ourselves. Everyone who seeks to tell another what is truth instead of letting him discern it for himself comes to stand between God and the person and in some way locks up their freedom.

This has been allowed for the sake of security in the past, but in these days as God speeds things up and His purposes start to be revealed for cites and nations, and the present truth challenges so many past interpretations of biblical texts, we have to be close enough to God to discern what He is saying for ourselves.

That may seem scary to some, while there obviously would be a "health warning" for immature Christians put on such electronic environments; such places do already exist and are working well. Anyone can come into the public areas of the digital neighborhood. There are also private areas of any neighborhood where only people with the right passwords, such as the apostolic and prophetic council can go.

Unearthing the Hidden

One of the difficulties citywide is the need for those who are currently unknown by the existing local church city leaders, to play their role actively in their calling to the city. Many people, who are called to be intercessors, workplace leaders, watchmen, evangelists, etc., are still in a place of obscurity.

Many prophetic voices worldwide have cried out that this is to be the revival when the unknown ones of God rise up to lead the way. How are they to be revealed? Existing city leaders have to be responsible for finding these hidden treasures and encouraging them to take their places in God's city plans.

Too often we behave like Egypt in this regard. Once we get to the top, as we call it, we suddenly become very protective and we set ourselves up as judges. We follow satan's lead and we recruit in our own image. Again and again we make ourselves mediators between man and God in the name of honoring our stewardship role.

But it is God who raises people up and He did not seek our agreement or judgment. If they are to be fully involved in citywide work, they must be recognized and released in their fullness. Not only must these people be sought out and found, but also existing apostles can follow God's leading to give place to what they are bringing to the city and further link it to all the other initiatives God is birthing at this time. The call is to work with the Holy Spirit to bring release, rather than, however unwittingly, organizing and controlling His work and hampering progress.

Help and Encouragement

We have seen that God works change in corporate environments through small units of transformation that we have chosen to call spheres of activity. These spheres work together through God's planning and guidance to bring change to the overall environment of the corporation.

Unfortunately, in most companies or cities these spheres can be quite disparate and have little or no contact with each other. Not all will be at the same level of involvement with God's purposes; some may not even have started working on their vision.

Individual spheres may be completely unaware of what God is doing in other spheres whose work is quite closely linked with theirs. Contact between spheres brings encouragement, increases understanding of the wider picture of what God is doing in their territory, and helps to speed up the work of God.

Of course there needs to be coordinated strategies for communications, especially ones hoping to cope with as diverse a group as the Body of Christ, but God is after all The Enabler. Suzie Hamlin, one of God's visionaries in this area says that "the introduction of systemized, measurable and sensitive communications mechanisms which deliver and share what is needed, and is of interest, will and does have an impact on attitude, methods of working, understanding, commitment and the perceptions of the people and their leadership." And she has confirmed it.

Called to the Workplace

Suzie Hamlin is one of today's citywide visionaries whom God has been training in the area of communications. Her area of specialization is in making information accessible across diverse people groups to facilitate and encourage greater productivity, stimulate fresh hope for the task ahead and get people involved.

She knows how to get the best out of people and has an innate grasp of what needs to be done to make information available to those who need it most and draw information out of people who have something to say.

From the time Suzie, as a very young Christian, first heard an apostle of God talk about business being a mission field, she knew she was called to that area. From that time she became convinced that God would place her in a significant place in business, and that she was called with the purpose of bringing about change within that business environment. Suzie was privileged in that as she shared her vision with her pastors, they recognized it was of God and did not stand in the way.

Her first job was in British Telecom Cellnet, the mobile phone/data side of British Telecom (BT), and she started in human resources (HR). She soon became aware that she would have an incredible training ground in the workplace, much greater than listening to teaching in the context of a Sunday morning meeting.

God started refining her immediately, as issues such as the fear of man and of failure quickly came to the fore and were rather painfully dealt with. Within a large corporation like BT, the HR function seemed to be very back-office and not really connected commercially so Suzie became very frustrated that she did not really understand the business.

At the same time, she also became increasingly aware that people worked in isolation, not understanding the context of the business they were in. As a result of these people working in isolation, through pride, apathy or fear, there was much wasted time, money and emotions.

One of the passions in her heart became to cut through this isolation and help people to find a sense of being a part of something and an understanding of the organizational structure and purpose.

She transferred into marketing, an area where she would begin to understand more about what was driving the business commercially, and also how it was structured. She had no marketing degree or any other relevant qualification, but it seemed an easy transfer when God made it happen.

Soon she became a program manager responsible for communicating internally and externally around product launches. She discovered that BT Cellnet was trying to sell its product portfolio through a sales force of about 7,500 people, selling everything from a handset to a very complex global data solution.

The sales teams ranged from global account managers dealing with global corporations to telesales dealing with handset sales to sole traders. She quickly realized that BT Cellnet was appalling at communicating with their sales force, and due to this poor administration was in danger of delivering product information direct into the competitors' hands.

Her passion about resolving isolation and improving how people communicate in the corporation and how each team works with other teams, came to the fore again.

She asked if she could create a way of communicating to that vast sales audience and she was given the job. Suzie found herself totally dependant on God, asking Him to show her how to share information across such a disparate and diverse structure. After extensive research within the various people groups, she developed a program called "Intuition," the objective of which was "to get the right message, to the right people groups, in the right media and at the right time, to deliver a measurable increase in sales."

The program was complex, utilizing a vast array of media dependent on the roles and locations of different groups, and very hard work. It seemed there was battle after battle over resources (e.g., people and finances), organizational restructures, internal politics, and changing business priorities, but God was faithful.

Gradually He gave wisdom and opened doors, changed decision-making processes, provided resources and made a way where there appeared to be no way. The program was met with great favor. It was as if God's order had come about and people recognized it as a better way.

As a result, it began to evolve and grow as people made it what they needed it to be. Intuition was also successful in business terms, as was demonstrated through research (e.g., from 21% awareness of product launch to 86% awareness within six months). But even more importantly to the business, it resulted in a measurable increase in sales.

Training and Consultancy

Suzie ran the communications program for two years and watched it continue to evolve and expand. During this time, she felt God wanted her to go as far as she could academically, while applying it to business. Despite the fact that Suzie knew she was not an academic, she felt that this meant a Ph.D.

God made it clear that whatever she studied He intended it to be central to the business she was part of, breaking ground in practice rather than theory. Therefore, It would not just be a qualification done in her spare time to obtain a title. As an employee in BT, she interpreted it to mean that she would research something that would break new ground for them in their marketplace.

Suzie therefore asked BT to support her to research why corporate businesses did not view mobility (and the use of mobile products and solutions) as being able to change their business into one that could be communicating 24 hours a day. In essence, what was stopping them from adopting mobility as strategically important?

The plan was for her to do this two days a week. She really felt that God was showing her how to sort out problems and stalemates within the business, and as a result she proposed that for the remaining three days a week she would act as an internal troubleshooter.

The research and radically new role were miraculously agreed to and signed off at the highest level, getting green lights all the way. To take on this new challenge, Suzie had to let go of Intuition, so she recruited and trained someone else to take it forward.

Then suddenly the move was blocked from within the company. BT would support her by giving her the money to study, but she would have to do it in her spare time. After many tears and much soul searching, and in the light of the way God wanted her to study, she knew that this was the end in BT.

Within a month of that BT decision, God miraculously opened another door to her. Suzie was asked to set up a business unit within a small consultancy firm, taking the thinking behind Intuition and developing it into a commercial model to sell to other corporate businesses. The main purpose was to create a way of communicating and sharing information that would enable their businesses.

Suddenly, after God had caused her to let go of all the insight He had given for Intuition, He directed her to take it back, but this time to envision a much bigger horizon. The consultancy firm also agreed to sponsor her Ph.D. She knew she was being released by God to pursue the communications passion that was so close to her heart and her research became a study into principles that would enable the flow of information around a large diverse structure, irrespective of the industry.

Joining and working within the consultancy firm was a baptism of fire. The day she accepted the job, the firm lost its biggest client, worth £1.5 million, and was traveling rapidly toward liquidation. They gave her the option of withdrawing, but she felt God telling her to stand with them at this time. She did and it was an enormous risk. The business was a mess and the support she received was non-existent, but God was faithful.

In 15 months she learned how to develop and launch a solution, get an understanding of the various organizations, and develop flexible systems of communications and training based on God's insight. In terms of business results, she won £600,000 worth of business.

She worked with companies such as Ericsson, Motorola, and others, including three large contracts in BT. Without God moving her, there was no way she would ever have had the confidence to be a consultant, yet God airlifted her into the consultancy firm and taught her how to do what she needed to do.

Fifteen months later, with the business sound again and making a profit, God led her to resign without any knowledge of what she was going to do next. She knew there was no way the company was going to release her naturally, and therefore God gave her the specific words to say.

God required her to find and train someone before she left, passing on all her insight and again giving up her model. God miraculously provided that person without her having to search for, ask or persuade anyone. She felt that perhaps God was asking her to set up on her own, but then fear set in. She didn't know where to start, she feared she wouldn't make the money, she knew she could not take any clients with her, and she knew she would not have a salary.

Then she was pursued again by another managing director from another small consultancy firm. The opportunity appeared to be from

God, and after much deliberation and prayer, she accepted a directorship with them at a starting salary of £65,000 and with a commission to help build their firm. But God wasn't part of it and she was fired four weeks before she started work there; humiliated and bruised she felt a bit like Jonah.

On Her Own

Suzie left her job on the last day of June and was meant to start the new role on the first day of August. God had already told her to take July off as a month of rest before the new job, and after she got fired He told her to still take it off. No clients, no business plan, no marketing and no income, but God said to rest and that now He was going to do it His way.

God told her He was going to bring the divine connections and open doors, bring about consultancy opportunities that were of Him, and she needed to discern whether they were of Him or not and only go through the doors that He opened.

God promised to be her marketer; He knew she had worked hard and now it was His turn. His way has been very, very different, and Suzie is finding that she has been totally detoxified from her old mindsets of business.

She has dedicated her business to God and is constantly on the lookout for His connections and the certainty of His timing. Just before setting up, she was approached by a group of Christians, within Leeds, who recognized that one issue across the city in terms of Christian community was communication.

God had spoken very clearly to them that there was great confusion, and the enemy really wanted to break down channels of communication. As a result of this she was commissioned to create a way of sharing information and insight and allowing people to find their voice across the city.

Although initially she treated it with a little contempt after resisting using her skills within a church context for years, God showed her that this was His connection, and His vision was not restrictive but diverse and fascinating.

God had originally said that her Ph.D. would be central to the organization she was part of and now it really was. Every time she considers the programs God is asking her to put in place, she finds herself also contributing to her Ph.D. There appears to be no separation and God is showing her His wisdom that truly will break new ground in terms of practice.

Miraculously, her tutors have said that her Ph.D. is her story and if she simply retells and reflects on that, she will have a Ph.D.

Suzie, knowing she had been called to business, never could see how children would fit into her lifestyle. The only business she knew was intense working within a corporate environment and then a consultancy firm. She had no desire to have children, could not let go of the vision, and passionately resisted any stereotyping she felt was so prevalent within church circles.

She had told her husband: "If God has called me into that I can't have children. Children would never fit with the demands of that working environment." But God has changed her, taken her out of the corporate environment, detoxified her thinking and set her up working in her community, where she is engaging with her neighbors, running the business from home and having a baby.

"And now He has done it, I can really see that none of it is in boxes, it's all united," Suzie says. "He's showing me how I can run a business, have a family, be engaged with the community and have a very successful marriage, and it doesn't have to be divided, it is only me that had it neatly boxed up!"

Network: Leeds

So after years of training in Human Resources, marketing and internal communications across large multinational conglomerates, Suzie has stepped out of her leading role in a knowledge management consultancy, and one of her first clients is the Body of Christ in the city of Leeds, England.

Suzie and the Network: Leeds team have been developing the program for 15 months, seeking to understand the shape of the Christian community, what information they need, what they have to say, and what methods of communication are currently in place.

Suzie finds that she has to do an enormous amount of research and ask numerous questions all over the city to really get the picture. Once this understanding starts coming into place, God then shows her how to navigate a way through to produce something that is systemic but also truly organic.

It is creating a way of sharing and connecting people across the city that is, and can evolve to be, what people need at the time. Initial research showed some generic results across all groups (e.g., wanting a monthly publication) but also specific results for how the program needed to be tailored for each organization (e.g., integration into their own internal communications to save on administration).

In terms of information wanted, there were ten top areas. Therefore, the program has been prioritized around these areas (i.e., prophesy, events, resources, mission and the nations, prayer children and family, youth and students, social justice, the spheres of the city, testimonies, and stories).

Research has shown that Network: Leeds must not be seen as an organization in itself and not something people are part of or not part of. There must not be a controlling center.

It has to represent the denominational mix across the city, and it has to be a servant to the city as a facilitator of communications and connections, bringing together those with similar dreams and visions. Suzie knew it was important to make sure they were not just communicating between individual churches, so within the pilot there are three churches, but also other citywide visionary projects.

One is called Youth Cells Network, where young people from across the city are networked into cells. The program is to help them communicate, share their vision and get more people involved.

Another one is called Prayer Strategy and is a network of intercessors. When serving church congregations, however, grassroots networking was a key and not merely communications between leaders avoiding bottlenecks.

The main purpose of the pilot has been to create a system and a backbone that works for a small group, but that has the capacity to go far wider. The core of the program is a highly adaptable and easily maintainable Web site, but the program is also tailored for those who have no Web access and need a hard copy.

The technology allows Network: Leeds to provide organizations with their own Web sites at a very low cost. These Web sites are highly dynamic, can look nothing like Network: Leeds and are entered via the organization's own domain name.

A monthly bulletin highlights the stories that have appeared the previous month and the events and prayer requests for the next month; giving a paragraph, it then allows people to read more of the story on the Web site or order it through the post.

Content comes in from all across the city as people who have something to say are signed up as information providers (e.g., Leeds faith in schools, people who do evangelism in schools and are providing information monthly on testimonies, job opportunities, prayer requests, events and other items of interest). There is no limit to how many can have their say.

One of the driving forces behind this communications program is to help various citywide projects or visions with their own communications. For the people who are driving citywide programs the system can be used to promote who they are, to solicit finances and to get people praying so that they are released to do the work they are called to do.

The communications system is aiming to provide information to connect people with similar hearts and to get information out there, where it will help and serve, particularly for those with cross-denominational citywide visions.

The pilot is already having a noticeable impact and now is the time to go wider. With all this in mind, Suzie is currently incorporating a wider group of ministries and churches in the project. The plan is that eventually it will incorporate the whole of the Body in Leeds.

As more groups are researched and start to engage, the shape of the program will change and evolve as their interests and visions will differ. The key is that now the backbone is there, the system can accommodate that change.

Pruning Is For Growth

The previous roles have given Suzie an amazing training ground, a real "boot camp," but now God is unfolding His plans and His insight. Suzie has been cut back in many ways, but the pruning is for growth. She is also helping me with getting some of the business communities I'm working with communicating.

Although originally Suzie was hesitant about working in a Christian environment, she now knows God wants to use her insight where He wants it. Suzie told me, "I haven't got the whole picture at all, but I feel more excited now than I did when I was earning loads of money and being very successful in the world's eyes, and I know God will show me the way as I step out in faith."

Revival—The Ultimate Transformer

Revival brings many challenges and raises many questions. We all think we want it and will love it, but while we may study previous outpourings, no one really understands it or can fully anticipate its impact on any of us.

When God comes to flood the city with His presence in revival fire, and prayer meetings happen daily in all companies, how will people know how to affect transformation? How will they know what God's ideal for a city or an organization is? Will there be as many opinions of truth as there are people, or will people grasp the truths hidden in God's Word? How is truth to be disseminated to the people?

I believe the only possible way that God can flood the city and house all the people He floods is right where they are now every day. There simply would not be enough room in existing static structures like local church congregational gatherings. There would not be enough leaders.

We need "Jesus is the answer" companies to be all over the cities, with people in them who can be coaches and mentors to those whom God is bringing into His Kingdom. We need good cross-city communications systems. Existing churches do not have the salaried and volunteer manpower to cope.

Imagine a church of 100 trying to cope with an influx of 3,000 passionate new Christians being added to their numbers in a day, like in Acts. Imagine the scene repeated all across the city. No one could cope. But out in the marketplace where Christians are scattered across the cities, those companies who have been prepared by God to take on and disciple their own employees, will be able to cope with God's new spirit-filled converts scattered across a wider area.

The models will be as diverse as the diversity of God. How the Lord reveals Himself to each of these organizations and structures will manifest the diversity He has determined will be in the Body of Christ and it will bring a greater reflection of Him in the city. The forerunners will be the ones that model the way to transform, as they will become the coaches and mentors to other organizations.

Preparing Resources

That is why we must be ready with the resource materials that are effectively discipleship programs for structures and processes and that will show the outworking of the change into culture and climate. God will have in place spiritual consultancies such as Corporate Transformations, and around the world other spiritual consultancies, able to go out as the demand increases. But when God comes like a flood I don't think any of us are going to be ready and I believe that the transformation of the Body of Christ will gather momentum when we can't cope.

Our experience is that when everybody has to run to try to catch up with Jesus, that is the most effective destroyer of existing mindsets and any strongholds of behaviors, attitudes, beliefs and desires, because we can't cope and we know it's God.

In the midst of that we have to be ready with the spiritual consultancies, internal and external consultancies that can be coaches and mentors. It is key for these consultants to not get in between the people and God. There must be no spirit of control. They will need to get alongside and selflessly sow in an apostolic way into the transformation of those organizations by the giving of resources.

It is a physical reality that the city buildings house the city. When the transformation is significant enough that the flood of God comes into those places and He pours out His Spirit on all flesh, what we'll see is the mix of the staff, between those who have come to faith in Christ and those who have not, beginning to change from a minority to a majority.

At that point we will see an increase of God's government through apostolic and prophetic councils and I believe at that time we'll begin to see all the elements of the Body of Christ—watchmen, intercessory networks, spiritual mappers, and the other roles God has breathed on over time—begin to have a greater priority than previously.

The organizations will click into gear and we will see discipleship programs rather than personnel programs or training programs, and an even more concentrated emphasis on God's character and patterns of behavior based on His principles, operating in greater measure across cities.

One Truth, but Many Reflections of Christ

I believe there is one truth, but I believe it will have many reflections of Christ. The outworking of that truth and the vehicle that truth is carried in will have many faces, many representations and many revelations. The outworking of it will be like God, infinite in its capacity for variety.

We're not going to be seeing a city of robots coming out with the same answer, but we are going to see the sum of His revival fire moving on those organizations, beginning to bring the fullness of His illumination in the city through the diversity.

Through all of it we see 1 Corinthians 12 expressed. It's only as we begin to get our mind around the sum of that in the city, that we will begin to get a glimpse of the sum of the illumination, the brilliance, the size, the variety, the height, the depth, the width and the breadth of God.

Disseminating Truth During Revival

Revival appears messy and uncontrollable. Indeed, every time man has sought to control God's revival fires, they have withered and died. Yet somehow truth has to be maintained, but legalism and control shunned. Once city organizations have undergone some form of transformation, even though it may not be complete, discipleship courses in the form of change management programs will be running, fuelled by case studies from the early adopters, who will be able to open their doors so people can see previously existing working models firsthand.

Resources Already Available

They will come to those who have been there before them, those spiritual consultancies God has already trained up to help them. They have all the apostolic and prophetic resource materials that people can take away and begin to implement the next day, to transform their organization.

The reason God is upping all the connectivity and all the desire to make the resource materials for transformation available all across the world, is so that more and more people will be ready, and able to go.

When they start to turn up in droves at the doors of those places God has set up as case studies, these companies and consultancies will be prepared with resources to equip them to cope with the situation they have been plunged into.

The drive of demand and the drive of God's Spirit together with the holiness and awesome power of God on those places, will be such a witness that visitors will want to grasp hold of everything God has taught these people, so they can get His destiny for themselves.

By this time, the digital neighborhoods and citywide communications systems will be red hot 24 hours a day as people clamor to draw off these Web sites. Years of preparation will be uploaded onto the WorkplaceMinisters.com Web site and other digital neighborhood Web sites and people will be able to download them any time of the day or night and print their own manuals.

One of the beauties is that even trainers in secular organizations can swap their ideology box and trade it in for Jesus' truth once they are born again, and can begin to be effective at Kingdom change management the very next day.

Linking to the Redemptive Gift

Another key area is revelation. We each need a good understanding of the part that we have to play in our city, territory, region and organization, which will draw on our specific redemptive gifts. As God comes and floods into a city, we are going to see revealed all the fields or spheres He has already planned and purposed, as referred to in Scripture, that go to make up a city. He has already planned and purposed that they be knitted together like a patchwork quilt across a city to give His Church maximum exposure in those places.

At that time we are going to begin to see our foundations and the generational inheritance that He has planned for us to have, take on a new level of importance, a new level of vision and focus in those organizations. On the one hand, there is the drive to equip those as He pours out His Spirit, but there is also going to be a drive to more equally play their part in the redemptive gift across the whole of the city.

At those times people are going to decrease so that the Lord can increase in that area. Leaders in their fields are going to subordinate their drive and their individual vision to play their part in God's plans and purposes for the whole city. Under God's unction they will sow their time, resources and energy in extracting the redemptive gift that has been placed on a city, territory or region.

This will begin to take a higher focus and we know that such sowing will bring a reaping for the region, which will cause all of the plans and purposes with which God has empowered their sphere to come to fullness. As they co-labor with God and the leaders of other fields or spheres, there will be a multiplication that's going to cause the fullness of the redemptive gift that God has put in the ground to resource the revival and God's transformation to the Church.

End-time Transformation

City and national transformation is driven by God and resourced and fulfilled by Him. It rises up from the roots of the nations spearheaded by those He is calling into position across the cities of the world. Just as revival is manifested by God alone and enacted by His grace, so transformation is brought about only by Him.

We are called to be stewards of His purpose, but the inspiration, planning and strategies are His. The privilege of living in these end-time days is awesome. We truly are seeing what many generations have prayed for and longed to see.

One thing is clear, God is releasing the vision in many to see their cities and nations transformed by His hand, and they are working toward that dream. Only a concerted effort and unity of heart and purpose brought by the Lord can bring about the atmosphere needed for change to be sustained.

The extent to which we can lay aside our own agendas and work with Him to fulfill His heart for us is the extent to which we will see real and lasting transformation brought about in our days. We may not be there yet, but already it has begun.

CHAPTER 5

Kingdom Coaching and Mentoring

"I am absolutely certain that this is a season of transition and in the midst of the destabilization of the culture that people are trying to hold on to, God is aggressively birthing a new thing. I am aware of the consequences of the destabilization, but I am vigorously running flat out with God to birth the new thing rather than waste time trying to patch up, prop up or salvage the old thing."

Arthur Burk

God is raising up trailblazers, people who are prepared to work outside the box because they know that is where He is calling them to be; people who get their legitimacy and finances directly from God. In the past the role of the Christian businessman was to walk ethically and to be sure to give plenty of money to the local church for the church to do the work of God. That paradigm has been smashed and God is driving home the direct legitimacy of the businessman.

Arthur Burk believes that God wants the two streams, church in the workplace and the Father heart of God, to merge and cause Christian business leaders to approach their jobs from a fathering perspective, nurturing their employees, not just exchanging labor for money.

God operating in the workplace never used to be a particularly contentious issue. In the context of Christian businessmen, there has been very little debate, but the paradigm transition to the new wineskin called "church in the workplace" already has been fiercely debated. We have business leaders pastoring, discipling and mentoring the people who are with them.

They are having evangelism and worship at work. When there are salvations, it becomes legitimate for a businessman to have baptisms and communion at work or even for a company to send out missionaries.

When God Moves, Somebody Always Contests It

The local church has operated as if it is the only structure positioned in society that has a God-given authority to collect tithes for the work of the ministry, to baptize, to give communion or send out missionaries. But it is actually God alone who can legitimize ministry and authority in any place (see 1 Cor. 12:4-7).

Entrepreneurship is intrinsic in individuals and they do what they are going to do without any legitimization. This move of God of church in the workplace is where Christian businessmen with an entrepreneurial bent begin to apply the "one another" verses of scripture in the context of the workplace.

God wants to redeem the workplace and to bring the fathering model back in this realm on a wider scale. The workplace is an area where men and women are positioned to father and invest in others in practical job skills, spiritual character and ministry.

Integrating the Body

This is not the end of the local church, rather it means a greater diversity of expressions of church. Unity is the key to moving forward with God and He has many ways of bringing His people together for a release of His purposes. Across territories the apostolic and prophetic councils are working for unity on a high level. But there are other ways I see God working, and real unity is a grassroots movement too.

As the citywide communications systems open up and churches start to communicate what they are doing for their people, the incubator church will be communicating what it is doing and the workplace church will communicate what it is doing also.

Similar concepts and ideas will begin to emerge, different types of church, the old and the new, will begin to see where God is leading them in the same way. It is through communication that the unity will come.

Only as people recognize and acknowledge the presence of God in each other that an honoring and expression of genuine love for each other in the Body will grow. One of the greatest causes of division in the Body is fear, taking the form of isolationism or elitism, with people guarding their own plot and trying to hold on to what they have. But as the existing Church looks at newer expressions of church and sees the hand of God calling them into being, our prayers are that their hearts will be moved by the Spirit and unity will come.

There will always be those who are so bound by their own fear and their own concepts of keeping what they have for themselves that they are unable to give and form relationships, even with those who have a passion for the same God as themselves.

But as revival hits the nations, as the Spirit of God is released in a flood across all the different city sections, the unsaved people will become less and less in number.

Unity can be ongoing through communicating. When the incubator church releases a representative into the workplace, they can maintain relationship with the local church where they had their roots, they in turn will establish wider relationships without competition. These grassroots level relationships will integrate the Body of Christ.

It is not for the new workplace church types to start a crusade to change the heart of existing church leaders, it is for the Spirit of God to do in the way He chooses. The new church constructs are open, to embracing relationships with existing churches.

No matter what form of church we are currently in, we need to discern what is and what is not of God. We need to reach out in love toward our brothers. Jesus said, it is by your love one to another that all men shall know you.

Church @ Work—A New Context and a New Environment

When God showed me how there could be city organizations reaching into the darkness all around, pulling people into the light, saving them, cleansing them, blessing them, and giving them freedom, I found myself weeping, so intense was the vision.

Only God can take a mammon-driven industry, remove the Babylon out of it, and put in the turnover, profit and heart, as we talked about in Chapter 3. It is up to us to grasp hold of the new constructs God is releasing, bringing His work to a wider playing field and making it more accessible to others.

As God has said, *"Wherever two or three are gathered together in My name, there I am."* Where people gather together, God joins in and places Himself in the middle of them. That is church. Just as Paul went into the workplace and built church around the people who came to him, so today's workplace apostles are doing the same thing.

Richard Nicol is building a form of church, and the presence of God is impacting the people he works with. Julian Watts is building another expression of church around the world. Many others across different nations are doing the same thing. They are building the Church where they are, because where the Lordship of Jesus is, His Kingdom can come. Where there are God-graced apostolic and prophetic foundations being put in place in the city, others will gather to be trained and equipped, and there the Church will be constructed.

The workplace church, or corporate church as I call it, is different from the local church in that it finds its expression across its daily life. It expresses itself in the way it carries out its business or workplace activity. It expresses itself in its relationships with its customers, its clients, its employees, its suppliers and the local community it serves.

It expresses itself by being a living witness because of the presence of God it carries. God is pouring out His presence into such church constructs. As God releases His revival, workplace churches also will see signs and wonders exhibited in their daily lives, as will local churches, and there will be miracles of healing. The workplace church has a much wider reach, as the average business contacts many people in its daily running. The result is that the more people you touch, the more miracles and testimonies there are, and the greater draw on others that you have, we will see almost a first-century type of church being expressed as God floods it with His Spirit.

It is up to the visionaries who called it into being to maintain the Christ-centered passion. The battles that affect church are just as prevalent in the workplace church as they are in any other church. You get spirits entering the organization, spirits who come to steal, kill and destroy, spirits who come to bring conflict and division.

Healthcare Practice

One example of someone who heard me talking about spirits in the corporation was Kate. She recognized at once that an Absalom spirit had got into her company. An Absalom spirit seeks, as a junior member, to flaunt itself and discredit the existing leadership. It is characterized by board-level takeovers and division within the company. Although she was in a small partnership, nonetheless this is what she was seeing.

Kate trained as a healthcare professional and worked in the National Health Service and Social Services in the U.K. and abroad. She became the regional head of services, and 12 years ago she felt God asking her to go into private practice with a Christian friend. She took a step of faith and set up a business partnership. The business grew steadily and God prospered them. They even had a part-time secretary and a part-time bookkeeper.

Enter the Absalom Spirit

When the bookkeeper left, a relative of Kate's partner joined them to help out with the bookkeeping. The relative had been in business and in the eyes of the world was much more experienced than either of the two partners in all aspects of running a business and had even advised them in the early stages of the business.

The three were close friends and the two partners trusted him. He seemed very committed to the business and gradually did more and more for them. Finally he was involved in all major business discussions and decisions, directly or indirectly, although he had no official status.

Kate then asked her partner for the business to tithe over and above what she tithed from her drawings. Her partner agreed and that year God blessed the business with a financial increase. The second year Kate's partner hesitated and agreed to seek God and study the Bible for a while.

She came back later and agreed that it was in the Bible. The business tithed for a second year and was again blessed financially. The following year the Absalom spirit had taken hold and the agreement for the business to tithe was discontinued as the partnership came under the spiritual challenge.

What we see here is two workplace kings and priests in a successful partnership and then a relative of one of the partners was brought into the business. With him came the Absalom spirit, which is the spirit of the boardroom coup. Kate thought all was well, as she trusted the friendships and the fact that her partner and her relative were Christians. But in letting go of her authority she had abdicated her kingship.

Gradually the relative started to increase his role in the business and the accounting procedures got bigger, although the client base was not increasing. It was at this point that Kate heard the teaching for workplace leaders about spirits in an organization.

As soon as she heard about the Absalom spirit, God highlighted to her that this was her situation. She had become increasingly uneasy about it and now understood what had happened.

The teaching advised not to directly confront the spirit by challenging the person, but rather to pray about it and get God's specific strategy for how to manage the situation.

For though we walk in the flesh, we do not war according to the flesh. For the weapons of our warfare are not carnal but mighty in God for pulling down strongholds, casting down arguments and every high thing that exalts itself against the knowledge of God, bringing every thought into captivity to the obedience of Christ, and being ready to punish all disobedience when your obedience is fulfilled (2 Cor. 10:3-6 NKJV).

She started to pray harder, repenting of abdicating her own kingship to the relative. She saw clearly now how he had taken legal control in the spiritual realm and she saw and understood the spiritual links for the first time.

Just as Absalom, King David's son, stood in the city gates at a rallying point and stole the hearts of the people, so the relative won the hearts of Kate and her partner. Just as King David left the city and Absalom took over, so in spiritual terms, Kate left her business procedures in the hands of her partner's relative.

Confrontation

At first Kate thought the prayer strategy was working, but then something happened that aborted it. Her partner needed a new car. Cars had never been brought on the business but had been purchased privately. Kate's partner asked to have a car bought for her by the company and Kate agreed to a car purchase out of her partner's share of the profits. It was agreed that the relative would research the purchase and bring the information to a meeting for a decision.

It was apparent that issues were being discussed behind closed doors and decisions made without consultation. Finally Kate was presented with the scenario that she was asked to sign a loan agreement for her partner to buy a car out of business funds. The car had been selected and the purchase agreement set up for a particular vehicle. Kate experienced real distress in her spirit and it was as if God was shouting at her not to sign.

She refused to sign the agreement that was in direct opposition to what they had agreed. She said she was happy to stick to the original agreement. It was at that point she took back her spiritual authority and territory.

Kate felt betrayed and hurt but she did not want confrontation with people she worked with and was friends with. However she knew she had to obey God and He was telling her not to sign the agreement. The confrontation exposed the damage within the partnership.

Break-up

The Absalom spirit did not like being opposed. Kate kept turning the other cheek and made sure she forgave each time. The intimacy of her previous relationship with her business partner and friend was under strong visible attack from that moment. Further out-workings of the Absalom spirit occurred, such as the removal of Kate's contact details from the business letterheads, which Kate challenged and the details had to be reprinted.

God told Kate to separate from business contact with the relative completely and that he should leave. Finally the difficulties of working in the partnership resulted in the ending of the nine-year business partnership.

Once the partnership was dissolved, Kate continued her business on her own. Since that time God has poured out His blessings on her business. She sub-contracts to three other people and God continues to bless her as she continues to tithe wholly from the business.

God's blessings have gone beyond an increase in the client base.

She receives settlement of all invoices promptly and few are outstanding. She has moved from being a sole trader to being a limited company. She now is able to run her business as God leads and is seeing an abundance and peace return to her business. The business is based on honesty, integrity and truth and God is with her to prosper her. God is encouraging her to train and empower others in her specialist skills.

Closer to God

The whole experience has compelled Kate to spend more time in prayer and listening to God. She is now closer to Him than she ever was. She has come to see that lack of prayer limits God's working in our lives. She has found out the need to push through the weariness and to find a place of perseverance and patience in prayer. She has also found the need to take time to seek God in every business decision. God gives the call, but He also deals with character issues in our lives. ·

Jesus called us to be gentle as doves, but cunning as serpents. Jesus' definition of "nice" is not the same as our worldly one. He wants to keep His people safe and protected. He has brought Kate through and is blessing her. God judges ungodly businesses and we execute God's judgment against interfering spirits.

The Workplace Church, Trading and Worshipping

Workplace church differs from the average local church in that it exists for the benefit of its employees, suppliers, clients and shareholders— its community. Its main reason for being is to fulfill the specific vision for the vehicle, that is to trade or provide services, and interact with its community. This is a key aspect. Without that it is simply a local church in a different place.

One of the main differences is that the workplace church will always seek to disciple the people within it to fulfill their own God-given vision, rather than to one church vision and to be released to set up their own independent workplace church to fulfill their vision.

The fathering workplace church will be available for nurture if required, but will not be involved in any decision-making relationship with its offspring. Workplace church therefore regards losing its key workers as a mark of success. It is not hooked on gathering greater numbers of people inside itself, but rather its whole focus is outward.

Another way the workplace church differs from many local churches is that it is not dependent upon the tithes and offerings of its congregation to fulfill its mandate; rather it is dependent upon its business success and the provision of God.

While it teaches its people biblical principles of money management and giving, it also teaches them to sow as, and where, God is leading them personally, rather than expecting all giving to come into itself. For example, giving of tithes to workplace churches allows for continued multiplication in the workplace and the city.

Part of its core value is to disciple the people within it. Its reason for being however is not just to work on them, but to fulfill that part of the redemptive gift God has for it in its field. It is also a vehicle for outreach into the community where it is based, and even wider, to express the compassionate heart of God to them.

The workplace church expresses itself in mercy movements as God leads it. It is a vehicle for giving the thirsty a glass of water, feeding the hungry and housing the homeless. In all those three activities they are ministering the gifts of Isaiah 11: healing and binding up the brokenhearted.

The vehicle for interacting with those constituents is the vision God has given them for their part of the workload. It is led by a workplace minister, who is an apostolic visionary refined and honed by God for territory-taking. Gathering about him will be fivefold ministry gifts with a commitment to serve the vision.

Its population may be large or small, but it is comprised of people who work for, or interact with, that business. Not all the people who work for the company will necessarily be Christians, but those who are will be speaking into the lives of their fellow employees, suppliers, clients and everyone they come into contact with in the normal course of their working day. Your trade becomes worship as you interact with your community for God's purposes. Jesus said,

> *"And I, if I am lifted up from the earth, will draw all men to Myself."* (John 12:32 NASB).

Church or Cell?

All of us carry within us, formed or forming, a vision for our own sphere of influence at work, but that does not mean we are all called to be apostles and build a church in our place of work. Many of us are called to be walking out our gifts and callings there, shining the light of Christ into our territory and fulfilling the vision He has imparted into us, but people based in secular organizations are simply not free to build a church where they are and still conform to company policy.

You could not, for example, divert company funds. Nor could you legitimately run discipleship groups during company time—you would have to do it in lunch breaks or after working hours. Yet you can still be filled with a vision from God for your department or company and be empowered by God to fulfill that vision, even though you are not building a church in the fullest sense, you will be bringing the Kingdom into that organization.

You can build a strong cell in a company with the full knowledge of the owner and you may even be able to influence the future of that company from the bottom up, but God is not giving full company resources to your sphere to achieve His plans and purposes. Cells form Kingdom expression in the workplace.

Already many are emerging. For those of you who know you are called to build cells in your workplace, take heart from Arthur Burk's story. His prayer and faithfulness to the Word of God increased the company profits by 300% in one year, and brought in a better quality of staff.

You can change the atmosphere of your department and you can change your company. You can bring in the Kingdom and create God's habitation in your workplace. It is from here through prayer that you can call out to the God who holds the heart of kings and turns them. It is from this point that God can get the secular owner to divert company funds to God's purposes and the owner may not even sense God's hand in what he chooses to do.

A workplace church does not look and feel like a local church construct placed within a company, but rather is integral with the company itself. It has a structure, an image and a purpose as one of the elements that make up a functioning city.

You can only run a workplace church if God gives you vision for that church, resources it, energizes it and motivates it. If you are free to fulfill that vision within the company policy, or if you are able to change the company policy to accommodate the vision fully; this is a workplace church. To set up and run a workplace church you have to be able to have the authority and freedom to follow God's vision. It's about taking land, inhabiting it, subduing it and populating it with people of like spirit.

The difference between walking out your gifts and callings wherever you are, verses running or pastoring a workplace church is governmental call. God's leaders are still apostles, prophets, evangelists, pastors and teachers. Although, it is usually an apostle or prophet that pioneers coming out of your current organization and builds a workplace church.

The Incubator Church

The incubator church is a local church that has a vision for equipping its people to go into the workplace and start their own cell or church according to their own particular personal vision or influence.

It is a preparation for taking church into the workplace. It equips the people to hear the voice of God at work, to help define and catch their own vision. It is a local center for destiny shaping instead of internal church programs. It is focused around releasing them into the fullness of their calling, which invariably will mean that they leave the local incubator church either to plant workplace churches or to carry out their own vision wherever that may be.

Some people may not leave the incubator church, realizing their vision is the training and equipping of others. And it is almost a mark of success of the incubator church that it sends out and loses its people, as it empties itself.

The spiritual principle of sowing that God has revealed in the Bible indicates that the more you give away what you have, the more God pours into you. The financial integrity to tithe back into the church of one's roots keeps the incubator church functioning and new people flowing in as God sends them to replace those ones who have left.

When the World Cannot Find Employment

Although the new church constructs are funded by those on the corporate payroll, these churches are able to work with all types of people to release God's fullness into their lives. God even has a vision for those considered unemployable, such as the injured, hospitalized, elderly and frail.

It is still the new church construct's responsibility to help them to fulfill God's vision, as there is no one unemployable in God's Kingdom. God has a field, a place, a territory for everyone. It may be that for a time or season they are nurtured, even hospitalized and restored, but God has a vision and purpose for them also. I do not believe God has a category of unusable people.

Kingdom Advice Centers

Kingdom advice centers are apostolic and prophetic resources. They do not have a permanent congregation. Most of the people who attend them will belong to some other expression of church as well. They are specialist resource centers to advise and help equip people for the workplace. As their name suggests, their primary role is to help advise others.

They provide a number of training courses, particularly hearing the voice of God in the workplace, to teach people to hear the voice of God speaking into their own personal life and work life. They operate training courses on how to find your vision and how to walk that out.

Many people have seen in their hearts what God is calling them to do, but they don't know how to get from where they are to what they are sensing. Kingdom advice centers help them find the steps. It's not that they teach people or advise them what to do, so much as helping people to hear the Spirit of God and find their own way forward through His leading.

Kingdom advice centers were started originally to help workplace apostles and prophets to realize their vision, but it has become apparent that more and more people from local churches are coming to be equipped to move into the area of the workplace.

Kingdom advice centers also provide resource materials to sustain apostolic and prophetic building strategies. These centers emphasize prophetic prayer and raise up and post watchmen all in a typical office facility.

Equipping and Freedom

The centers also work to bring new levels of freedom to the people who come to them by restoring healthy foundations through spiritual cleansing, counseling and restoration; providing freedom from curses, ungodly beliefs and hurts. They are specially equipped to deal with specific deliverance issues.

They run seminars about transformation strategies for corporate entities, cities and nations. They are equipped to help people to flow with the Holy Spirit and bring that divine balance between two types of advice: workplace competence and prophetic thrust.

The centers give mentoring and prophetic counsel by not only bringing the Word of God into business, but also demonstrating how to grasp and implement what God is actually saying through the Word. Analysis of the prophetic word and guidance is also provided, and where appropriate, they will provide coaching and mentoring.

These networking centers are for Christians in the workplace and they prepare some people for ordination as workplace ministers. But mostly, they train those who are transitioning into incubator churches. They are happy to confront the demonic in the workplace, giving strategies and tactics to conquer, subdue and bring peace to each territory.

We did some work with Ron in Texas electronically. He responded with this revelation, "I received advice from God, through people I didn't know, in some other part of the world, as if I were there. There are many people just like me all over the world that need what the Kingdom Advice Center offers."

Kingdom Advice Center in Action

Nick worked for a computer software company but felt God was asking him to leave and set up his own business in order to provide a channel for wealth into the Kingdom. He realized that he needed to work with God in order to accomplish this, but didn't know how. He had learned about God's financial economy, but there was no help available specifically for Christians who had a vision for business.

He kept asking God for contacts that would provide help in realizing the vision. Then after eighteen months, someone in the Church invited Nick and his wife, Kitty, to a meeting for Christians in business. He didn't know what to expect, but as he walked in he experienced a spiritual dynamic he had not seen before. He was amazed at the worship and the way the prophetic gifting was used to speak into people's business and workplace callings. He knew at once that this was what he had been looking for and that God wanted to use this place to train and equip him.

First Steps

Through training at the Kingdom advice center, Nick learned how to receive words and pictures from God and he began to develop a confidence that he could hear from God at any time and for any situation. He learned to recognize that inner witness of God speaking to him.

At first it was challenging and he had to learn to build up courage in what he was hearing, then learn to act upon it and respond to what God was saying. It wasn't always the obvious business decision; in fact to Nick's thinking, it was often the reverse. He had to trust God in new ways, but the Kingdom advice center was a safe environment in which to learn. It was also a place to receive personal prophetic words from others that provided a continual source of encouragement and insight.

In sharing these experiences with Kitty, together they learned how to weigh what they heard and understand more about the timing of the revelation received. Sometimes it would be an advance warning, sometimes an encouragement to press on, sometimes a directional word and sometimes a revelation of who God is, but it was always relevant in the business context.

They also learned how to go back to God once they had received an initial revelation and ask for further detail, as well as how to understand more about where prophetic words end and wishes begin, as many people take prophetic words and interpret them wishfully through a lack of understanding.

They also found that as time went on, God would not only give them both a sense of what He wanted to say, but would also give each of them a different part of the plan, like pieces in a jigsaw puzzle. As they shared with each other what God had showed them, the parts would fit together and give a more complete picture.

As a result, they found that God was working with them in parallel, using each to crosscheck the other, resulting in greater clarity of revelation. This was a starting point in learning how to run a company God's way.

Using Prophetic Revelation in Business

Having learned how to hear God, Nick and Kitty began to use this to make business decisions. Nick was seeking additional business and felt the Lord direct him to contact a particular company. The company was very receptive and proposed a project for which some budget had recently become available.

Having prayed about how much to charge, Nick submitted his proposal, giving the figure that God had shown him. To his amazement, this turned out to be exactly the amount which the organization had available in their budget, thus securing the deal.

At the Kingdom advice center, Nick also learned that God assigns fields of harvest specifically to each business. It was of prime importance for him to identify these fields and work together with God in taking these areas. He began a process of asking God to reveal these fields and the revelation received began to shape the company's direction and decision-making.

Nick's business provides solutions for automating business processes. It covers implementing technologies such as document management, workflow and electronic forms. God had begun to reveal an idea for a new product that was to form part of their field. As Nick was praying about the design of this product, God showed him a picture of the universe and impressed upon him the need to understand something of how it works.

A discount bookstore came to mind and when he went, Nick bought a book that illustrated the universe. The information provided gave him a different viewpoint on the design of the product and some of its basic structure.

Spiritual Warfare

In working out the vision God was giving them, Nick and Kitty began to encounter spiritual opposition. However, the teaching they received at the Kingdom advice center combined with the prophetic gifting, they could begin to discern when spiritual opposition was being encountered. They knew how to hear from God, how to counteract it and then exercise authority in the spiritual realm. In one situation, difficulties were encountered in securing business from a company, but as they prayed God gave them a picture of a glass dome over that organization.

Nick realized that this represented the enemy's defensive layer and rule over the organization, but that the glass was fragile and could be easily smashed by the hammer of God's voice. As they prayed this through and declared God's Word, they sensed that breakthrough was being achieved. In the following months, step by step, pieces of business were released to them.

On another occasion, God warned Nick and Kitty that the enemy was seeking to hinder them from securing future business. Concurrently, the Kingdom advice center started teaching about the weapons available in God's armory for waging spiritual warfare. So Nick and Kitty asked God to show them how to overcome the enemy in their situation and what weapons to use. In one instance, Nick saw a prophetic vision where he was taken to meet The Landowner. The Landowner showed him a map with clearly marked boundaries. God showed Nick a room full of swords laid out on tables and showed Nick one particular sword. God told him it was the one He had chosen for him to use. It had a lion's head on the handle and a blade that wasn't made of metal. God was challenging Nick to take up his full warrior authority.

As Nick wielded the sword and spoke the Word of God, with 1 Samuel 17:45-47 as the basis, he sensed the enemy being removed from the land. About a month later, two significant business deals were obtained that moved the company on to a new level.

Worship—The Core of It All

Worship is a theme that God continues to remind Nick and Kitty about. It causes them to focus on God as the center of their lives, rather than on the business. It enables their hope to be renewed, their faith to be stirred and their hearts to persevere in order to see what they have been promised come into their experience.

God showed them that the altar of worship would allow His glory to dwell in the midst of their business and everything they did. Worship helps them to be detached from the pressures of situations and enables them to see circumstances from their Father's perspective. It is intimacy with Him that God desires more than anything else and He showed them that worship not only glorified Him but it also was a powerful weapon of warfare.

God Works on Us as We Worship

One time during worship God gave Nick and Kitty several pictures. The first was of a car windscreen covered in dead insects after a long journey. They felt God was saying that the dead insects related to things that were hindering their vision. The second picture was of a funnel used to pour liquid into a smaller container. Liquid was being poured at a great rate into the funnel but relatively little was flowing out of the narrow bottom.

A few weeks later, the Kingdom advice center began teaching about how to deal with issues that hinder God working in His people and their visions being realized. It covered such topics as sins of the fathers and resulting curses, ungodly beliefs, soul/spirit hurts and deliverance from demonic oppression. Through these sessions many issues were resolved in their lives, a greater unity was achieved in their relationship, and they were able to move on to experience a greater measure of God's flow in their lives.

Kingdom Finances

Although they had received excellent teaching from their own church in the area of Kingdom finances, at the Kingdom advice center, Nick and Kitty were encouraged to combine this with prophetic revelation. Weekly, they were challenged in a positive way to ask God where, and how much, they were to sow their finances.

The first time this happened, Nick asked God where to sow and God told him to sow £2,000 into the ministry of a couple in their church. The next Sunday at church he went up to this couple and gave them a check for this sum during the offering time. He was amazed to be told that they had just sowed into the offering a check for £200, thus resulting in an immediate tenfold return.

They have often found God taking them on adventures in their giving. On one occasion God told them to sow into an organization. Shortly afterward, they found that the gift had arrived just in time to finance a conference for Christians in business that God had called them to arrange at very short notice.

On another occasion God led them to sow money into another couple. Later they discovered that God had instructed this couple to empty their bank accounts as a step of faith before going to a conference in America. On their return, they discovered Nick and Kitty's gift in their post and yet again discovered God's faithfulness to them.

Not the Only Way

Just like Arthur Burk, Rich Marshall, Ed Silvoso, Oz Hillman and many others, I see God's initiatives in the workplace, not as being a replacement for traditional church, but as enfranchising the world through the workplace church, to reach and nurture what has become the biggest forgotten people group.

I see it as being God's plan to maximize the redemptive gifts He has placed within cities, and a strategy of fulfillment and freedom for those vast numbers of people who live and work in our cities but are largely untouched by church as it currently expresses itself.

God's thrust into the workplace has been gathering momentum and He is currently releasing much revelation to workplace people about how He wants to use them in the times that are coming. I see it as being God's natural way of funding His Kingdom projects, and releasing freedom for the underprivileged, broken and damaged people who are always on God's heart of compassion.

I have spoken in this chapter about three different types of new church constructs that I am currently working with. They are not, and will not be, the only types of expression of new church types. God is infinite in His ways and wherever people gather together, for whatever purpose, He will find a way to build His Church among them.

CHAPTER 6

Purpose and Destiny

This section of the book is personally for you. It is to rekindle new life in you and raise fresh hope. This is to help you grasp hold of the reason why you were born. It is about Jesus reaching into your heart to bring forth that hope that cannot disappoint. This is to show you that He is establishing your destiny and giving you the power, the energy and the motivation to help you reach that destination.

When God created this world He had a purpose. Somewhere back before time began, the mighty Creator God devised His plan for this earth and for every individual being who ever has or ever will live out their lives here. He brought together a rag-tag group of individuals, a jigsaw puzzle of variety, and saw a purpose for each and every one of us. He has planned a purpose for us, not just for eternity, but also for our lives here on earth today.

Of course God doesn't see us as a jigsaw puzzle like we do. I think God knows the shape of His end-time Church intimately. But because we cannot embrace the fullness of all God has going on, it has to look like jigsaw puzzle pieces to us. Though it might look disconnected and mismanaged, I believe God is very controlled and precise in the way He's bringing all types of people to work together. That's why it has to be only Jesus and the Holy Spirit who does it.

We are not disparate, random people separated from each other by time and geography, but we are by His hand a living river of destiny flowing on through the seasons and generations to bring His plans to fruition, that His glory might be revealed upon the earth. We all have our purpose to play in preparing the way for the Lord to return in the power and awesome splendor of His Majesty.

Locating Destiny

My job, the sphere where God energizes, resources, purposes and helps me fulfill my destiny, is to come alongside God's visionaries and show them how to walk out their destiny. It is my personal command from God. It motivates me and often exasperates me, but it fills my heart to see people locate their destiny and help them to get moving along the path toward their destination. And I will work day and night to help them because that's the passion God is pouring into my sphere.

All of us have a destiny to fulfill. Some have an apostolic or prophetic call upon them and carry the mantle of governmental authority for building churches; others are given different gifts and calling, but all are called to find and grasp hold of that vision from God for which He designed and created them.

Every one of us is included and all of us have a reason for being born on earth. So how do we find out what God has for us personally? How do we catch our vision? Where do we locate the place of our destiny? It might be right under our noses.

Destiny—A Call From God

Destiny comes from God. It's His supernatural plan for us and we can't expect to understand it in the natural. The outworking of our destiny will be hands-on, down-to-earth practical, but the origins are in the supernatural heart of God and it's only through the supernatural working of the person of the Holy Spirit that we can grasp hold of it.

Appropriating the vision for our destiny always comes by revelation. Our destiny is not for us alone, but it is part of our membership ministry in the Body of Christ. It is to fulfill God's purposes for the earth and our personal destiny is just one part of that giant jigsaw puzzle.

People usually come to me at the stage when they have seen something of that vision, but they only see fragments of truth and they don't know how to progress with it. Others may have a wider grasp of a specific calling, they just need someone to set their feet on the path and help them see how to start walking from here to there.

The initial stage involves getting the prophetic spirit flowing in people and helping them to catch the supernatural flow that God releases when they ask Him about their destiny. The start of fulfilling their destiny always come through revelation and when God imparts the understanding that He has called them for a purpose, He also imparts faith for that purpose and a passion for it in the core of their being.

Destiny fills a hole and gives you a reason to pursue Him, and it gives you a passion to fulfill His purpose for you and to know Him better and love Him more. Destiny is the single answer to the apathy that lies rampant in so many of our lives today. It's challenging, awesome and mystifying, but it grips your heart for Him and gives you a reason to dare all for His purposes.

Flowing With the Holy Spirit Within

The key to finding and fulfilling your calling is becoming close with the Holy Spirit. He is the one who gives us unction. He is the releaser, anointer, guide and revelator. God in the person of the Holy Spirit is the One who will guide us into all knowledge and open our eyes to His plans for us.

He is the One who will make a way and teach us and train us until we are ready to be released. Then He will release His anointing upon us in even greater depth than we ever had before. He is the One who will bring us all we need to find and fulfill His purpose for our lives.

The only way I know how to flow more deeply with God is to go to those who already do this, and to follow them as they practice doing it. Then we are working through Matthew 11:29, in which the Lord says *"take up my yoke and learn of Me."*

Learning to work with the Holy Spirit means attending workshops on how to do it. It means joining peer groups that sharpen each other, and networking with other students of the spirit. It means creating an environment, even a digital neighborhood, where people can fire questions at each other and share experiences.

Learning to work with the Holy Spirit requires the kind of schools where people learn to practically work out such issues. It requires some safe havens where people are in an incubated environment to get going after crossing the Jordan into the Promised Land of their destiny. Always, the Holy Spirit Himself is the best teacher.

Obedience Releases the Flow

Learning to work with the Holy Spirit and to draw forth God's leading, God's vision and God's empowerment is done through God's grace. You start the process of learning with the Word, which imparts faith into your heart. As Hebrews 5:14 says,

> *But solid food is for full grown men for those whose senses and mental faculties **are trained by practice** to discriminate and distinguish between what is morally good and noble and what is contrary to divine or human law.*

The Word is the starting place of training our senses and God promises to train us. Earlier in that same passage, it reads in verse 13,

> *For everyone who continues to feed on milk is obviously inexperienced and unskilled in the doctrine of righteousness, which means of conforming to the divine will in purpose, thought and action.*

With reference to the divine purpose God has put in us, if we are unskilled in how to conform to that in thought and action, we remain infants, not able to talk yet. We need to practice flowing with the Holy Spirit to grow and mature in Him so we can grasp hold of our destiny.

In John 15:14, God says,

You are my friends if you keep on doing the things I command you to do.

It is an amazing thing that God is prepared to call us His friends, but there is a condition:

If you keep on doing the things that I command you to do.

The things God commands us to do are the things that are going to help us achieve His purpose.

To clarify the relationship further, God emphasizes that He is not calling you to be a slave. He says in verses 15 and 16:

I do not call you slaves any longer, for the servant does not know what the Master is working out but I have called you My friends because I have made known to you everything that I have heard from My Father. I have revealed to you everything that I have learned from Him. You have not chosen Me but I have chosen you and I have appointed you and I have planted you that you might go and bear fruit and keep on bearing, and that your fruit might be lasting that it may remain and abide so that whatever you ask the Father in My name, as presenting all that I am, He may give to you.

God shows us in these words that when we choose to work and head for our destiny with Him, that He calls us His friends. But the condition to being His friends is that we do the things He commands us to do. Yet not as a servant and not as a slave, but as someone who is looking to work out those things God is showing us so that we can achieve His purpose in our lives. Notice the Lord says, *"You have not chosen Me, but I have chosen you and I have appointed you and I have planted you."* What that speaks of is your destiny; that you would be fruitful and fulfill God's purposes for your life.

Our Most Intimate Friend

So how do we move forward and become mature? God promises to send us a Helper and it all starts with being His friends. The first thing we have to do therefore is to learn to hear what He commands us to do. We need to learn to hear, to know, to see and to sense what our Master is doing, because the Lord says He has made known to us everything that He has heard from His Father.

To do that, we need to learn to hear with spiritual ears, to see with spiritual eyes and to sense with spiritual senses. So how do we do that? The Lord says that He has given us the Holy Spirit, which He calls the Comforter, the Counselor, the Helper, the Advocate, the Intercessor, the Strengthener and the Standby.

It reads in John 16:7-8:

I will send him to you to be in close fellowship to you and when he comes he will convict and convince the world and bring demonstration to it about sin and righteousness, uprightness of heart and right standing with God and about judgment.

What the Lord is promising here is that the Holy Spirit will come into close fellowship with you and convince you what is good and what is not good. He will do that by giving you the training of your senses that we heard about in Hebrews 5:14.

The Holy Spirit begins to work with us in training situations, and the more that we are prepared to listen to that inner spiritual unction, the more we begin to get revelation and illumination and the more we begin to know about things we haven't understood or thought were important. It is a process, and the process is accelerated by our attending workshops, but our own personal response to God is the key to learning.

When I first started, I promised God I would not do anything in the day without talking to Him and asking Him, but I'd get home in the evening after work and find I had not spoken to Him all day.

How can we be sure the Holy Spirit has been given to us to help us walk in such a close personal way? There are many promises in Scripture that teach us so. Repeatedly the Bible says the Holy Spirit, imparting and opening up the Word, will be a light unto our feet. As the Holy Spirit motivates us to read parts of His Word, it will give us the answers to what the next stepping-stones are.

As Joshua is trying to move forward with the Lord into the Promised Land, the Lord gives him the greatest bit of advice any of us can have on this walk. Joshua 1:7 reads:

Only you be strong and very courageous, that you may do according to all the law which Moses My servant commanded you.

For us as Christians today, the day-to-day guidance of the Mosaic Law is supplemented by the leading of the Holy Spirit. We should allow the Holy Spirit to guide us through direct revelation and through the Bible, where we can find God's spiritual principles that are particularly relevant to our specific stage of progress along the journey to fulfilling our destiny.

As it says in Joshua 1:8:

This book of the law shall not depart out of your mouth, that you may meditate on it day and night, that you may observe and do according to all that its written in it. For then you shall make your way prosperous, and then you shall deal wisely and have good success.

The Holy Spirit guides us into the part of the Word He wants to talk to us about. This is not like a law or book of rules, but it is a relationship with the Holy Spirit. It is He who teaches us, guides us, counsels us, comforts us, exhorts us and motivates us to study scriptures and discuss the truth with Him.

God is helping us so that our way to destiny may be successful, it may be prosperous and we may bear fruit. The central part is that we can't allow the Word to depart from our mouth for any part of the day or night because it is the central way in which the Holy Spirit communicates with us.

Logos and Rhema

Revelation and understanding comes from studying the Bible. The Bible speaks to us as the "logos" of God, or the written word of the Lord, bringing direction and training in all things for everyone. But the Holy Spirit also speaks to us through the Bible as a "rhema" word, or the spoken word of God, quickening and bringing supernatural unction, revelation and discussion with us about a particular part that is for us in our circumstances right now. He highlights a particular point for our next step on the path and He begins to quicken and make it alive to us. Gradually, step-by-step, God begins to give us revelation and illumination.

Paul's Prayer

In Ephesians 1, there is a prayer from Paul, who knew the Holy Spirit well and knew that the Holy Spirit brings revelation. He prays for you, the individual reading this book: "For I always pray to the God of our Lord Jesus Christ, the Lord of glory, that he may grant you, a spirit of wisdom and revelation, of insight into mysteries and secrets in the deep and intimate knowledge of Him, by having eyes of your heart flooded with light."

It is the Holy Spirit who floods the eye of your heart with His revelation and His light so that you can see your next step, your next strategy or your next tactic. You can see the next place to buy, the right time to sell, the next step to move forward in your call with your family, and the next move into what the Lord wants you to do and have purpose and passion for.

He promises to bring that light and knowing. Paul prays for you to have the eyes of your heart flooded with light, flooded with knowing, flooded with understanding, so that you can know and understand the hope to which he has called you—your divine destiny; your place of being and purpose, the place that God has created you for.

In this place of destiny, you will come to know and understand the immeasurable and unlimited surpassing greatness of His hand on your behalf. He is able to demonstrate in you, working through and for you, what His mighty strength is.

Whether your concern is a person, a vision, a family, a business or a school, God is able to bring his power into those situations through the Holy Spirit, who leads us and teaches us, so that we can understand our purpose.

Key Scriptures for Hearing God

Throughout the Bible, God makes it clear that relationship with Him is the key to progress. This involves a growing awareness of His character and person, and it involves talking to Him and hearing what He says in reply. The Word shows us that it is God who leads us forward in the right path.

It is Proverbs 16:9 that says,

A man's mind plans his way, but the Lord directs his steps and makes them true.

Proverbs 20:24 says,

Man's steps are ordered by the Lord how then can a man understand his way?

And Jeremiah 10:23 says,

I know the determination of the way of a man is not in himself. It is not in man even a strong man or a man at his best to direct his own steps.

It is as you study the Scriptures, these and many others, that you begin to make the transition and trust the Lord for guidance. Although God could do it on his own, and just put us where He wants us, instead He wants a relationship with us. He only works with us through different levels of relationship.

He accepts us where we are to start, but expects us to grow and move into deeper communion with Him. God wants us to love Him and to have friendship with Him. He doesn't want to direct or tell us, He wants us to explore a relationship as we walk out our call. If we have no walking/talking fellowship, we don't have much of a relationship.

We may have faith but we won't know we have purpose and we may end up not fulfilling our purpose, because all personal prophecy is dependant on our choices. As Luke 6:46 says,

Why do you call me Lord when you don't do what I ask you to do (Author's paraphrase).

We are dependant on God and as long as we are trying to get there through relationship, He will ensure we get there. If we have no fellowship, He just keeps trying to get us to adjust our position and come into alignment with what is best for us. In spite of all these scriptures it is possible to miss our destiny if we do not work with Him as He directs us.

Obedience Is the Key

Again and again it all comes back to hearing His voice and obeying His command. In Psalm 37:23-24 it says,

> *The steps of a good man are directed by the Lord when he delights in his way and busies himself in his every step. Though he falls he shall not be utterly cast down for the Lord grasps his hand in support and upholds him.*

If you decide to go and use your own mind and your own behaviors apart from God, you become deceived, and if you turn aside and serve another god you will have problems. The conditionality of serving God is at every turn. I believe God did that as a mercy to us because all of us begin to rely on ourselves as soon as we think we can.

As Psalm 37:5-7 says,

> *Commit your way to the Lord....He will make your upright-ness...go forth as the light....Be still and rest in the Lord.*

If you don't rely on Him He won't bring it to pass. He meets you where you are and then begins to give you higher vision. Once we are in relationship with Him, talking to Him, listening to Him, doing what He asks us to do, He will pull us through to fulfill our destiny.

Talking to God

Once we understand that God wants to work with us through relationship with Him, we will want to talk to Him, and pursue that relationship. What God wants with us is a two-way conversational relationship, not a silent one. Although we are now expecting God to talk to us, we also will be talking to Him.

It is a question of balance, as it is in all relationships. Prayer, talking to God, is the core of working with the Holy Spirit. We do need to ask for things and our Father is delighted when we ask. However, He is especially delighted when we ask for Him to fulfill His purposes through us. We need to be asking God what His will for us is, and how He plans to fulfill that will and purpose through our lives.

If someone came to me saying they had no idea of their calling, I would start with prophesying the word of God into their hearts and letting God impact their hearts with His destination for them and then build off what God says. He energizes, resources and gives plans and purposes to that, and then stands alongside while they learn to walk forward in it. God will spark their desire for destiny by telling them what His heart is for them and where He wants them to go. It is God Himself who ignites destiny in their spirits through faith imparted by the prophetic word.

I would then expect them to ask God for further revelation and ask for confirmation from the Holy Spirit. Working with God is just that, it is a working with, not only expecting God to make things happen to us. We work with God as He comes alongside us and helps us.

Personal prophecy is never fulfilled by our attempts to do so in our own strength and planning, but is invariably conditional upon us being obedient to working with God, listening to what He is saying and working through those things with Him.

Finding Destiny and Working With the Holy Spirit to Put that in Practical Terms

As I have said, I always start with revelation. Put people in front of a company of prophets who can prophesy to them, and that ignites destiny in their spirits. That gives them a broad scope into it. Then we have to give them understanding of the elements of destiny, the biblical view.

Even with those who are cynical, I would start by letting God hit their spirit with a good prophetic word. If we can speak vision into them, faith will be ignited. They should come to a company of prophets in their nation to have that flame lit within them. I believe

God has got safe places opening up that people can come to for prophecy. People have no problem going on training courses for work, so why not come and have destiny ignited in them by the prophetic word.

We teach that vision emanates from God and the supernatural context of vision. Then we take them into the supernatural and practical expression of gathering together all the elements of destiny and vision, and we help them discern the difference between their own thinking and what God is motivating in them.

We end up with a first-pass document that covers their environment, mission, competencies, anointings, core value of their ministry vehicle, prophetic words spoken over their destiny, calling that others see on their life and their own communications with God. The Lord then takes over, releases more revelation and the people get very excited about their destiny. Probably the biggest cry from the majority of Christians today, is that they want someone to help them confirm their destiny.

Waste Howling Wilderness

I believe people should take the time and spend the money to invest in their future by traveling to a reputable prophetic company in their country and hearing what God has to say to them. If you are unable to invest financially, for example if you are penniless and jobless and cannot afford the ticket, I believe that God is more interested in moving you into your destiny than you are.

I have a wealth of testimonies of God working with individuals, bringing people across their paths, bringing resources into their hands, moving on the hearts of leaders and making it possible for them to attend conferences with a gift, such as getting pound notes through the letterbox.

A prayer to God is all that is necessary to get you located in the position where you can receive all that God wants to get to you. I don't believe there is any limit to the poorest person who gets a copy of this book in their hands. They cannot be in a worse place than Deuteronomy 32:10, which says that God found us in a howling wilderness and He enveloped us, encircled us and held us as close as the apple of His eye.

There is no one who gets this book that can be in a worse place than a howling wilderness. God is able to pick them up, keep them safe and secure, deal with their foreign gods, lift them up and ensure that they get in front of the right people at the right time. For the price of a phone call or a text message, we will believe for God to hook you up with someone who will start working with you. Go to Workplace Ministers.com for our contact details.

Checks and Balances

In working with the Holy Spirit, it is our relationship with God and our regular communion with Him that will provide the most sensitive check of where we are going and whether we are on the right track. We are all human and everyone can be deceived so it is good to have others bear witness with us that what God is saying is on course.

Outside prophetic input can also be valuable. But the biggest check is from the Holy Spirit Himself. If we are not following the course He has for us, he will often withdraw our motivation, or withhold finances from us. Such challenges do not necessarily mean God is calling us to attention, but often they do. Closeness and intimacy with Him is the greatest place to find confirmation that we are on or off track.

As we come to work out our vision in more detail, we will find there are other checks to the questions we must ask ourselves. Counsel from wise friends can also be good at challenging us. But at the end of the day, other people cannot see the hope we see, because our destiny is given to us alone to fulfill.

When a Man's Destiny Changes a Nation

As a Christian steward, Hans Neilsen Hauge had a national perspective to his thinking, as he had his eyes fixed upon the whole of his nation of Norway in the 19th century. He knew the biblical principles of success and he preached them with fervor.

"Nature itself teaches us that we should work for the things we need for living. Experience teaches us that doing nothing is the main reason for bad behavior," he said. His teaching and preaching challenged people's attitudes to the extent that they were willing to accept the challenges and break with their traditional way of living.

Hauge wanted the believers to begin all kinds of business endeavors, which would bring financial success and break the yoke of poverty. Then the people could be free of those who were oppressing and controlling them by their financial strength. Wherever he went he was always looking for natural resources and opportunities that could be used for developing businesses: waterfalls, farms, minerals and fishing.

Whenever he found what he was looking for, he talked to his friends whom he thought were capable of buying and developing it. His followers, who often had backgrounds as poor farmers, eventually became wealthy, forming a new generation of leaders. They were famous for being hard workers and never giving up. Sometimes they would buy a place that no one had ever been able to run successfully and after a time of hard work the place would prosper.

By the age of 33, he had started a mining industry, several paper factories, grain mills, a fishing industry, farms, shops, publishers and printers, cotton-finishing factories, crafts, trading companies, shipping industries and salt boiling plants.

He also was the most-read author in Norway in his time. He wrote 37 small and large books and sold 250,000 copies altogether. They were full of fire and written in a language that people understood, penetrated with a living Christianity. Those books were important tools to spread the revival and make it deeper. The thoughts and attitudes that filled the books became the people's accepted way of thinking.

He also communicated through letters, counseling others in business and spiritual matters with valuable information and ideas. He was arrested for his faith 11 times, the last time spending ten years in prison, where his health was almost totally destroyed. But he did not give up, he simply used the time to write more.

The results of his life included an industrial breakthrough, 20% of the population getting saved, a radical change in moral standards that penetrated society, an improved productivity on farms, an increased participation of the laity in politics, and an interest in learning among farmers and their employees.

The Haugians became the elite in their communities and the most trustworthy, successful and informed citizens in their nation. The Church also was renewed from the inside, as the nation's first missionaries were sent to Greenland and Norway sent out the most missionaries per capita of any nation at the time.

It took about a hundred years for Hauge's breakthrough work to be acknowledged and honored publicly, but in 1996, the king, parliament, church leaders and the nation celebrated the day when Hauge was baptized in the Spirit, acknowledging that he was the reason for Norway's transmission from poverty to wealth.

He was the leader that built Norway spiritually, socially and financially, and by combining all those elements, he changed the nation inside-out. Hans Nielsen Hauge was just one man, but he was a man who walked with God and found his destiny.

Destiny's Position

We will find our destiny in our membership position in the Body of Christ. God is building up His Church to change the world. We will do nothing for Him and His purpose outside of the Church. Destiny is from God; it is supernatural.

If we have in our sights a calling that can be achieved in our own strength, then it is not the fullness of the purpose God has for us. Standing secure in Him as Lord and Master, as part of His Body, we will find that which he has destined for us. We will find our destiny, our calling, from that position of security in Him.

God has destined His Church for eternity, but destiny doesn't just come. It is tied up with our level of maturity and with timing: God's timing for us, our growth cycles and God's timing for others with whom we will interrelate as we fulfill our destiny.

Timing is a key element and we can't force it. We need to be ready when He is ready. We are given a window of opportunity to be ready at the right time. However, if we feel we have missed our window of opportunity, we don't need to worry and give up, we simply need to repent and pray. God is the God of the second chance and He is a God of grace.

It is through the grace of God that we will fulfill our purpose. We will not find it by our own strength. We will not find it by our own determination. We will not find it by rushing out and looking for it, or by setting up connections and making a way for ourselves, but by the supernatural working of the hand of God.

Ruling and Reigning

The next thing we have to understand is who we are. God hasn't called us to fulfill our destiny as just a random gift that He would give us. It is part of the outworking of God's purposes here on earth. And we must understand that in order to fulfill that, we have to take up the fullness of our positioning in Him.

The Word says we are to rule and reign with Christ forever. I am talking about grasping hold of the fullness of the authority that He has for us, and realizing that we are seated with Him in heavenly places.

We are in a race and every one of us is being cheered on, as it says is Hebrews 11, by a mighty throng of people who have gone before. The race is to fulfill our purpose and to take up the crown of glory He has for us. But we don't want to think of the race in normal terms.

In Ecclesiastes 9:11 it says: *"the race is not to the swift,"* so we can't think of the race in terms of human speed; "nor the battle to the strong," so we can't think in terms of human power and strength; "nor bread to the wise," so we can't think in terms of human wisdom; "nor riches to men of understanding, nor favor to men of skill, but time and chance happen to them all."

Our destiny will be won for us on this earth and we will fulfill it in very practical ways: in our place of work, in our community, in our family. We have to understand God's wisdom because only God has the spirit of excellence that is required.

In order to grasp hold of our destiny we need to see it from God's perspective. Not to say, "I'm going to be the leader of a large company, so I think I'll buy a large house and an executive jet with all my money." As we look at it from God's perspective, our hearts are changed. It is not only our purpose we need to see from God's perspective, we also need to understand the game that we are playing.

We need to know the rules of the game. We need to know the relative strengths and weaknesses of the other players. We need to know what rights they have and what rights we have. We need to know what sustains them and what sustains us. And we need to put the whole thing in the context of the times and seasons of God.

Hands-On Destiny Worksheets

As I have said, finding your personal destiny all starts from revelation and relationship. It's God's life-guiding mechanism that He has designed and tailored specifically for you. Most people think it just happens; they don't understand they're working with God throughout their whole lives to bring them to a position of achieving their purpose.

What I do, as a destiny counselor, is to give sense to people's life leading. It's happening anyway, but for most people it's all mixed up with things they don't think God is involved in. By the time they've finished training, they're saying, "God was involved in every area of my life, before I was even born again. He's putting the skills in me, I can recognize where he's anointing me. I can see what the vision is."

Once they get to that place, they have the skeleton to hang the rest on in a more purposeful way rather than just finding out after it happens, and they can actively work with God toward His purposes for them.

When I'm working with someone to determine their calling, I'm listening to what God is saying all the time, as well as what the person is telling me. I bounce off their responses and listen to what God is prompting me to ask in order to draw out what else they have been in training for by Him.

Destiny Step Plan

To do this on your own, look at the headings in the questions and write down all the answers that come to your mind. Start with prophecies and other communications over you and your organization. Then write down what others see in your life or organization. Don't think of this as a form-filling exercise, it is a "dreaming with God" activity.

When we are looking at destiny there are some practical questions we need to ask ourselves. Although we can answer some of the questions in the natural and it is right that we do so, and while those who know us best can answer some of the questions for us and that is helpful, there are also many aspects of our destiny that can only be answered supernaturally and we have to work with the Spirit of God to have Him reveal them to us.

Destiny Chessboard Diagram

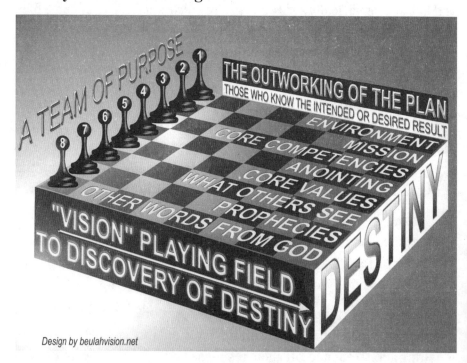

Design by beulahvision.net

There are eight different questions that we have to answer before we can work with God on the finer details of discovering our destiny.

Destiny Questions

1. Environment

One of the early essentials you need to know from God is where you are to fulfill His purpose for you. "Work" is too broad a sphere to home in on. Workplace environments are as varied as we are. The marketplace involves anywhere where people are. But the environment where we are to fulfill God's calling on us is not simply a place.

It also involves the environment where we are based, all the associated interactions that go on there, the atmosphere and culture, those people we are to interact with, and the technology we use to interact with them.

To gain some concept of these things we need to sit down with God and dream a little. Dream of where He is taking us. Is it a geographical place, a conceptual place like "the media," or a people group? Is it global, is it for our workplace, community, church or city, or is it something we see but cannot localize?

God is asking us to dream for Him. He wants us to be dreamers for His Kingdom, to give Him the time to stir up His plans and purposes for us. If He's calling you to trade with Africa for example, ask where in Africa. What are your boundaries? Where are you to start? Are you called to trade across the whole continent, or just to one particular nation or city, or to a specific designated area?

There are also aspects of the internal environment of where God is taking you and your organization. Where it is to be based is another one of many questions you need to spend time seeking answers for.

Asking the Lord for the answers to these and other questions is His will for us, so don't be afraid and think you should already know the answers, or be directed by other people, or follow market trends, or make your own decisions alone.

You do have to make your own decisions, but only when God has given you the raw data to work with. Unless you have heard from God, you are working in the half-light with blindfolds on.

Other aspects of internal environment include knowing your market and understanding whom your customer is and why he is your customer. The technology you are to function with and communicate through is also a vital part of your internal corporate environment, as is the team you are to work with.

Are you founding an organization or working within an existing company? Is the organization staffed by Christians, unbelievers or a mixture of the two? What kind of a team are you to build, how large is it, how is it structured, what kind of ethos are you to establish among them?

Do you know who they are? Are they all in one place or are you multi-centered? Using our example of trading with Africa, how many people will you have in your home base and how many in Africa, or will you just travel and do it all yourself as a one-man band?

If you have staff in Africa, will they be nationals or are you planning to settle your own staff there? What is God saying to you about all this? Because you can be sure He has an opinion on it all. This is His plan and His purpose we're talking about. Who are the key players who will support you? Who will be praying for you? What level of prayer is needed to start the thing off and what level needed to maintain it? What is God saying to you about all of this?

2. Mission

The next thing you need to talk to God about and dream with Him about is your mission. You may think you have an idea of your mission, but you need to get specific with God about it. Defining your mission will tell others what your organization, or you personally, consider a meaningful outcome. It will point to how God is calling you to make a difference in the economy and in society generally.

Returning to our example of trade, what are you to trade with and in? What are the results you are set up to achieve? Why has God called you into trade, what is His purpose in this, what Kingdom objective will God achieve by having you trading with Africa? How will you impact the environment and society you are trading with? What impact will you have on the economy of the area or nation you are trading with? What is the purpose you believe God has for doing this?

Back to our trading example, the mission could be: "To set up a series of trading centers across Africa in order to provide outlets for the local people to sell their goods in the West for a fair price and thereby to increase the prosperity and independence of the local people."

Or it could be: "To print training materials and set up a school in a little village in Mozambique to improve the education and therefore the prospects of the people." It is good to remember that we are called to a servant-hood ministry and that part of its fulfillment will bring blessing and enhance the lives of others in some way.

3. Core Competencies

Your core competencies are your life's experience. Even if you are straight out of school you will have acquired plenty of them on your road through life so far. These are natural life skills, which God can take and use for His purpose. Maybe you ran the school newspaper and discovered how to gather stories, how to meet deadlines, how to interview people, how to use computer layout software, etc.

God has put that experience in you. By the time you've reached adulthood and perhaps raised a family and held a responsible job, you have many life skills that God has been training you in. Maybe now you are unemployed, considering yourself unemployable, and thinking even God must have given up on you, but I've got news for you.

You are loaded with core competencies. This is probably the very time God wants to pick you up and start you over. He's been training all these life skills in you for years and now He's just about ready to call you out into the field for Him and enable you to use those skills He's been working so hard to ensure you acquire through His guidance of your life.

Maybe you're a young mom with toddlers and staying at home, thinking destiny for you is nappies and bibs and nothing else. Well you're wrong. Just because you are in a season of raising your children right now, doesn't mean God has nothing else for you.

He is preparing you for it at this present moment. He's loading you up with core competencies: caring for others, running finances, disciplining your day and cooking meals. Young moms with more than one child are brilliant at multitasking.

Maybe that dream you thought God put on your heart seems just too far out there to be real any more. If it is from God, it's not out there at all. The preparation is what you are going through right now. That's how He does it. He works on your daily life experience to build the necessary skills in you to enable you to fulfill all He is asking of you.

And don't think, maybe it will come to pass when the kids grow up and leave home. It starts right now! Don't worry about the anointing, that's His part and He never messes that up, it's your skills He needs to work on and that's exactly what He's doing at the moment.

Maybe you have found yourself in a dead-end job, hating every moment and looking for some hope in the future. God has His awesome hand on you and on your present situation. Talk to Him and ask how He's using your present experience to grow these essential life skills in you. He'll tell you, and the answer will probably surprise you. If you don't know how to hear His voice, get yourself fast to some place where you can learn it.

What skills have you had managing people, directing projects, fathering, preaching? Whatever you have done, you can be certain God will put it to good use when you cross over your Jordan and step into your Promised Land.

4. Anointing Assumptions

The anointing assumptions are the spiritual gifts God has given you, your gift mix. Every one of us has a different gift mix, all deliberately tailored toward our destiny and purpose. Many people know their anointing mix and are working with God to enhance their fluency in these areas of anointing.

Preachers need to practice preaching and getting revelation from the scriptures; motivational speakers need to keep letting God inspire them; counselors need to gain experience and pass exams; finance directors need to know how to hear God with regard to wise investments. The list is endless.

Of course your anointing mix may not be what you or others are expecting. If you are anointed for the workplace, as most people are, you may find yourself fulfilling a pastoral role, or a teaching role in your company, without even realizing that you are anointed by God to do that.

Maybe you are a doctor or a nurse, and you find that after you have talked with a patient, that person is encouraged and starts to believe they will get better. That can be the anointing of God upon you to encourage or raise faith in people. God's anointings are His equipment for His purpose and they are as varied as His purposes are. Maybe you are bringing apostolic governance to your company, or speaking words of prophecy or wisdom into your boardroom straight from the heart of God.

Traditional church thinking has confined God's anointing to fulfilling a role in the local church. Some may, but many more will be anointed by God to deal with their everyday situations at work and in the home. So not only do you have to know what your anointings are that God is bestowing upon you, but also where they are to be used, and how.

Now Check the Fit

At this point you need to check that they all fit together. Don't worry about how or why, just look at what you've assembled and see how it all fits together. Do your assumptions about environment, mission, core competencies and anointings fit with your natural and spiritual realities? The nearer you are to stepping into your destiny, the nearer the fit will be.

If there is a large divergence in some area, you should talk to God about it and ask why. It may be that you are thinking along the wrong track, or that there is another dimension of calling He still wants to release to you, but He hasn't discussed it with you yet.

How does what you have answered to these questions fit with what you believe God is calling you to do? Do your giftings fit with the requirements of your sphere of service for the Lord? If you are 58 years old and tone deaf, it is unlikely God is calling you to be the next sensation on the youth music scene!

It sounds foolish, but we all have our own foolish dreams. Yet as we look at them in the light of our anointings and competencies, we can usually identify quite easily what is God's calling and what is our own fantasy.

5. Core Values

Our core values are our internal standards for which we are willing to expend or gather resources. What are you passionate about, what do you hate?

Maybe your core values are to motivate love for Jesus in everyone you meet. Maybe it's integrity in finances. Maybe it's that you are passionate about ensuring the underprivileged have an equal chance at education and to go to university.

Even outside biblical principles, we all have a set of core values that are specific to us, and our calling. Are you passionate to see the media challenging the morality of political decision-making, are you motivated by in-depth political discussions?

6. What Do Others See in You?

What are the qualities your friends see in you? What are your natural gifts and abilities that are already manifesting at work, at home, among your friends? Do they see you as having a financial bias? Do they see you as having great patience for training beginners in information technology?

Are you a facilitator in their eyes, or a serial entrepreneur, or do they see you as being a good communicator with kids and youth? The people we live and work alongside know a lot about us. Their opinions are valuable in helping us to determine where our gifts and callings lie. They are not the only indicator of destiny, but what they see in your life is significant and helpful.

7. Prophetic Words

What are the prophetic words spoken over you or your organization or workplace? This is probably the easiest place to start, but it can also be the most misleading because often you are trying to interpret what the Holy Spirit has revealed without a proper context.

Prophecy only reveals in part, and the Body of Christ is littered with people who have had their hopes dashed either because they were unable to properly interpret the prophecies spoken over them, or because they did not understand that most of personal prophesy about the future is conditional.

There have been many books written about interpreting personal prophecy, and when looking at your personal prophecies, it is helpful to read one of these books. We have to interpret what is spoken over us in the light of our yieldedness to God in all areas of our life, in light of the seasonal variation of our life's progression and to establish the contextual relevance of the word to our particular environment.

It may be for a time not yet come and for things we have not yet embarked on. It is good therefore to interpret prophecy with caution when seeking to determine the calling God is leading us into. It is also good to remember that what the Holy Spirit has spoken to us, He can interpret further for us if we earnestly seek Him for guidance.

8. Dreaming With God About the Shape of Your Destiny/Company

This is not to express your fantasies, but to seek God for how He sees your destiny. It is a Holy Spirit-led activity. Is your destiny to be second-in-command in the division of your company, or to build a company of your own? Are you called to leave your current place and nature of work to get a new job in a different nation, working with the AIDS victims in Africa, for example?

Or will your current company fund you to do this? How are you to get there, what steps is God taking you through to realize this? If He's not talking to you about how He's planning to do it, about the shape of it and about the season you are currently in, then you must pause and ask why. God is a God of confirmations, but so often we seek to have our fleshly thinking confirmed instead of His will for us.

Working on a Destiny Blueprint

The final part of destiny is to put us into what God is doing in the territory. If we focus on a situation, how do we progress it. What is our part? What is the organization, the structure, the process, etc.? God may be speaking into many spheres in our life. How do we know we are on the right track?

It all comes together. It's like the coordinates of longitude and latitude; when they meet, it gives you the point you need to be at. All the eight elements form a grid; they come together to pinpoint the coordinates of your destiny.

How do you know you're in the right place when you are at sea? You take a point from that lighthouse over there, on that bit of land here and from that star over there and from the longitude and latitude and any other significant points you can see and it all comes together to pinpoint where you are.

So, with answers to these questions, all the boxes fit together and are mutually confirming. That's how we spot the difference between what comes out of your own spirit and what comes out of God's.

In your own spirit and flesh there may be many desires, but you won't have been experienced in it, you won't have been trained in it, it won't be the thing that fits in with all your other gifts, it won't be in prophetic words and you won't have words from other people about it.

Sometimes people don't prophesy over you until you are on course with your destiny. Why? It's typically because it is God who gives prophecy and He waits until you are ready to receive what He has to say.

Another reason is that you may not be going to prophetic watering holes, or you may not be open to the prophetic, or have closed it down, or abused it. It may be you simply don't know about the prophetic, but at Kingdom advice centers you can come and begin to partake of the prophetic flow.

What other people see in your life may be prophetic or may be natural. I remember one man who chased me around the world and when he caught up with me he said, "you're the only finance man who can help us here." I'm not even a finance man! He saw what God wanted him to see, and he wasn't even a Christian. The dreaming is very important because you're giving God an opportunity for opening you up and expanding you for seeing what God sees in a way you haven't necessarily been trained.

With all these eight areas you are able to pinpoint your destiny.

Heritage Center

Dave and Sue have a vision and they know how God works throughout your life to bring you all the experience you need to fulfill His purpose. They have a vision for a heritage center, a cultural center that raises awareness of Middle Eastern culture.

They want to teach about Jewish roots and give people the Hebraic overview of their Christian faith, how Jesus was a Jew. They want contact with schools as well as churches. It has to be open to the public, and have a hospitality aspect as well, including a coffee shop.

Dave used to work for CMJ, Churches' Ministry to the Jewish people. They were also in St. Andrews (Chorleywood) under Mark Stibbe's ministry, where the church has a real heart for Israel. Dave has done museum exhibition work and is experienced in teaching adults and school children.

His original background was as an environmentalist. Dave is coming at the project from the museum curator point of view because that's his background, whereas Sue is coming at it more from the people point of view because that's her background.

Sue has experience with working in the community, she's a people person, has worked in social services and has done catering and food. She's interested in the culture and the people. God is using the acquired skills of both of them to teach and reach the man in the street in a culturally relevant way.

Initially Sue felt the center was just one of Dave's good ideas and didn't realize it was God-breathed. But as they sought God, the calling to teach about the Jewish roots became very clear to both of them.

Realizing that people don't typically pick up large books and read about theology, they realized they could communicate the Bible best through museum-style exhibitions. Not stuffy and old fashioned, but culturally relevant. For Dave and Sue, dreaming with God was not a day of dramatic prophetic revelation, but a growing awareness of God's purposes for them. They came to know that this was God and that He was passionate about what He was calling them to do for Him.

At the moment, they are developing the teaching resources. They teach about Passover in churches, and teach about marriage from a Hebrew perspective, linking it with Christ's relationship with the Church. They have many props, including a Bedouin tent that they use to explain about the life of Sarah and how she trusted God for the fulfillment of what He had spoken to her.

God has really circumcised them. He is moving them to a new territory on the other side of the country. They have had to sell their house and are not going to be able to own a property right now. They are learning to depend on God every moment.

David has always had a secure job and in many ways their security was in that and not in God, but now they are learning to depend on Him and not on themselves. It is a big step of faith for them to move to another city without a job. Most people depend on the state and on their jobs, not on God, but Dave and Sue have to lean on God and not on their jobs.

They understand they should only do what God is doing. Sue points out you can have a vision and think, "we'll go and do it." But God says, "No, not yet, just that bit for now." Gradually the thing grows, but it has to be done in God's timing.

Moving On

One of our goals is only to do what we see our Father doing. Our best example of that is to look at Jesus. He is our model, our goal and our hero. He's the best salesman, the best purchasing director, the best everything.

If we could do that, we'd make fewer mistakes, wield more power and be more successful. We are to go and preach the gospel and disciple nations. Filling the land with people of God's Spirit and working with the Lord to bring that group of people into a greater reflection of Christ individually, corporately, citywide and nationwide.

As we do that, we are also being prepared for eternity. We don't go floating around the world as intergalactic vagabonds; the world works and it has a purpose. If we are walking out our individual destiny and the corporate vision of our field, that is preparing us for ruling and reigning with Christ.

The purpose of doing the destiny exercise is to give you the basic spheres God is calling you to add to. It provides a sheet that acts like a plumb line to help you know where you are and what phase God is in with you: whether He's dealing with sin, teaching you to ride in the high places, how to turn on more rain, or whether you should just be standing on the word and waiting for divine appointments.

So you've seen your vision. You've caught the fire of it and you're excited. It's all there in front of you. The prophecies make sense and other people are confirming what you see. It fits with your core skills. It's bigger than you ever would have conceived on your own, but you know it's God and you know He's going to get you there somehow.

You can just hear those clouds of witnesses in heaven cheering you on. You're prepared for it, come what may. You know this is what you were born for. Faith has risen up inside you and you know by God's grace you can do this. The Lord's hand is strong upon you and you're ready to go. But questions remain: How do you step out into your vision? And what can you expect to happen when you do?

CHAPTER 7

Vision Strategy and Tactics

Opening the Flow

Empowerment is about opening the flow of God. It is about seeing and embracing your vision, and starting on the journey toward your promised land. So how do you go from having seen your vision, which is too big for you to possibly fulfill under your own steam, to actually fulfilling it? How do you walk out this call?

All of us have a vision from God, everybody has something that God is calling them to do, but as we come to know and grasp hold of the significance of our calling, our vision increases and increases, like ripples on a pond when a stone is thrown into the center. God reveals more and more to us and we come to realize that things are not as we had imagined originally.

So, you've seen something of your vision. It may be just snatches of it, or it may be that you have quite a well-formed concept of it. The first thing you need to do is to home in on the geography of it. Where is your promised land? It may be conceptual, it may be geographical, but that promised land is something you have to grasp hold of.

It is something that, like Abraham, Moses and Joshua, you have to put before your eyes and live with. It's no use thinking, "I'm going to do that one day," and then walking away from it and getting on with your present life and forgetting all about it.

You have to walk in that juxtaposition, that time of pain between the nearly but not yet, seeing your calling and knowing that you are nowhere near working it out. Watching time stretch and wondering why God was so excited to tell you about it when He is taking so long to get you there.

You have to live your present life experience to the full, walking out God's purpose, and at the same time grasp hold of where He's taking you. Somehow you marry the two together; this only comes supernaturally and it only comes by the grace of God.

You have to look with the eyes of the visionary at your promised land. You need to be praying for it. If it is a physical geography that you can easily access, you need to walk on it, put your feet on it. You need to hear what God is saying to you about it.

You need to ask Him about the times and seasons and what you still have to learn, and He'll tell you. Once you have learned how to work with the Holy Spirit, how to hear His voice, He will lead you and guide you, for it is His promise as long as you are obedient to Him. If you ignore your promised land by putting it on one side and assuming it will happen one day, you could well miss out on it completely.

The first thing you have to do to grasp hold of His promise to you is to pray about it. You need to come to God regularly in prayer about the vision He is holding out to you. You need to cry out for a deeper infilling of the Holy Spirit. You need to reach out to God and ask Him how you prepare to get there. **The first stage of any preparation is always prayer**.

Initially, when you have just seen your promised land you will not yet be a sphere of influence. You won't yet be in that privileged position of God providing all your resources, all your motivation and all your energy. God won't be carrying your risk for you yet, because in the early stages of vision there is no risk.

The risk begins as you put your feet upon the road. You need to see the vision and keep it alive in prayer. You need to claim it by speaking God's promises and standing on them. You need to remind Him that He has shown you this vision, that its of Him, and that by His hand alone it will be brought forth. You also need to seek further revelation and ask how to proceed.

Empowerment is related to growth, maturity, faith and intimacy. It has to do with grasping hold of what God is showing you and believing it. You need to speak out the promises of God until the "rhema" word of God raises faith in you to appropriate it and prepare for it.

All vision has to be appropriated by faith before you can actually be released to do it in the natural. Grasping and appropriating vision is not a passive thing. It is an active thing. Just as vision only comes when you get close to the Holy Spirit, so vision is only walked out by an ever-deepening relationship with God.

With our spheres, the major input into the early stages is prayer. Prayer is what we need to ground the vision and prayer is what we need for further revelation. Prayer and waiting on God is how we understand each step of the journey, that, and obedience to what we hear God telling us. Vision is a supernatural gift from God, but in the early stages we start to walk it out in the natural through prayer.

Much of opening the flow has to do with preparation and walking it out in the natural. As God comes to test us He will take us deeper and deeper into a relationship of listening and obeying Him. Like Ezekiel's river, we walk first ankle deep, then knee deep, then deeper and deeper until eventually we are swimming in God.

During this time, He comes to us and deals with all our false mindsets, all those times we have ungodly beliefs, where we have misunderstood things about His person, about our calling. Step-by-step, He comes to undo what the world has formed in us and then to put His mindset and His beliefs inside of us in order to prepare us.

He comes to break us apart from all our foreign gods. And one-by-one He dismantles our inner mindset of wrong beliefs and understandings and takes us along a path until we are ready to cross the Jordan and step into our promised land.

The Foes Against

Although we may see God's purposes for us in our hearts, between God in the third heaven and us here on earth, there is the second heaven inhabited by demons who work against us. So we will find as we attempt to walk out our destiny that we are confronted by opposing forces.

We will be opposed where we live, but the good news is that there are also angels who were not cast out of the third heaven because they remained pure and good, and who are on our side to help us to find the way forward.

It is only by revelation that we will get the understanding of what our destiny is. And it is only by His supernatural intervention and guidance that we will make it through to fulfill it. As we saw previously, if we are listening to Him, obeying Him and seeking Him with all our hearts, we will find Him and He will put His hand upon us and carry us through. All He needs is our commitment to be obedient to Him and to love Him and serve Him.

To consider the wider aspects of destiny, its origins and fulfillment, we need to look with greater clarity into the three heavens as described in the Bible. Let us now examine the three heavens, and bring them forth into greater clarity to consider where destiny is created and by whom, and see who is working against it happening and from where.

Figure 1—Diagram of the Four Dimensions of Reality

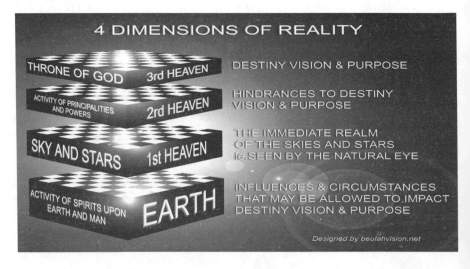

The earth is the realm in which man operates. We also see here the activity of spirits and other influences and circumstances, which may affect our personal destiny. The first heaven comprises the sky and the starry heavens. The second heaven is the realm in which are based the principalities, powers, rulers of darkness of this age and spiritual hosts of wickedness in the heavenly places.

According to Ephesians 6:12, the third heaven is the realm from which Jesus rules above all things. We can see therefore that the real power base that controls the heavens and all the earth is the third heaven. But here on earth, we are called to stand against the wiles, the deceptions and the temptations of those forces who seek to deceive us, that they have the upper hand, just as they did when they tempted Jesus.

The battleground on earth is the souls of people, who are largely oblivious to the battle. Certainly most have no idea that they are partly hindered by the second heaven and influenced by both angelic and demonic groupings on earth.

Destiny and Freedom

As the diagram shows, we have angels working with us, and demons working against us. So we will find that during our walk toward our destiny, God will be dealing with things within us, where we have strongholds that are not from Him.

Strongholds include sin, thoughts, feelings, attitudes and behavior patterns that are not of God. They also include mindsets that are contrary to the will of God and worldviews that are from a different perspective than that of God.

There are many, many things that God will start to free us from in order to bring us into a greater level of release. The walk into our destiny is also a walk into our freedom. God wants relationship with us and He also wants to bring us into our personal fullness.

And while He wants to bring us into the destiny through which He will fulfill His purposes, He also wants to bring us into personal freedom so that we can become closer to Him, because the things that bind us are also the things that limit our relationship with Him.

So the walk into destiny is also a walk into deeper levels of personal freedom.

Time and time again I have seen how as people walk into their destiny they hit stopping points beyond which they are unable to progress. That's when God, through His mercy and power, sorts out another issue in their lives. They walk into a greater level of freedom and only then are they able to take hold of and follow the next step toward their destination.

Qualifying for Promotion

The level of freedom we have reached in the Lord is related to our vision and destiny. With each new step the Lord leads us to, for an expansion of vision, there comes a greater liberty because He sets us free to be able to work in that next phase. He walks hand-in-hand with us.

God brings new liberty through deliverance. This is a key part of how we walk forward with the Lord. There are a whole group of people who don't understand that, so they don't understand why they're not walking forward in their vision as they desire. In reality, they are actually constrained by not having enough liberty on the inside of them.

Wrong mindsets and evil oppression or possession are the root of so many anxieties, panic attacks, and of much sickness and disease. Yet it can all be dealt with in a walk with Jesus. He wants you to have liberty from all abuse, including sexual abuse, physical abuse and substance abuse.

There are healing rooms around the world springing up as more and more Christians grasp hold of God's grace in this area. They are not just for spiritual deliverance, but also for counseling wrong mindsets, healing soul-spirit wounds and bringing release from the pain of the past.

As an example, Chester and Betsy Kilstra are pioneering visionaries in developing apostolic training resource materials to raise trainers and safe places where people can have demon oppression and possession dealt with. They too have heard God about what He is doing in the marketplace and have produced materials tailored for God's workplace visionaries.

I know many personal stories of how God has met people in this way. My wife, Pauline, and I can give testimony in that area. God did not let me do what I'm doing now until He'd dealt with spirits of rejection and failure hiding behind stuff that had happened to me through my life.

Families of a Visionary

Pauline's fear of walking alongside a visionary, and the sacrifices that had to be made, is also very important to understand. We were in the middle of the Markets Unlocked situation and I couldn't talk to Pauline about walking alongside my vision, as she got ill. Then one evening she woke up and saw a shape and a light and thought it was an angel.

The angel said "Do not fear" and she just said "alright then" and turned over and went back to sleep. Since that moment, everything that would have gotten her knotted up before just goes over her head now, and doesn't touch her. It was what enabled her to walk forward.

The partner's point of view is a major consideration with visionaries. There were many days when my wife was just sobbing. But since that time, God cocooned her and nothing touches her. The impact on the family is significant. God won't allow things to move on until He's brought all things back into a workable relationship.

A good example is that of Dr. Hamon, when he finally bought the land for Christian International to build their headquarters. Dr. Hamon's testimony was that he had felt, and the prophetic words had agreed, that they were finally getting their field for a base facility, but it wouldn't come together.

They had paid $40,000, but the rest of the money never came and the land was defaulted. It left him sore with the Lord on this topic. In the process he found out that his daughter was really struggling at college and was heading toward a breakdown.

He had not been able to hear her voice crying for help because he had been so absorbed in his vision. His understanding was that God allowed him to lose the land so he could stop and, with his wife, nurse his daughter back to herself.

God is not beyond holding up progress on our vision because of a situation in our family. It is an important part of our understanding that God can redeem time with our families and our vision, but He calls the shots about when He does this. God came through for Dr. Hamon and now there is the awesome CI headquarters facility in Santa Rosa Beach, Florida.

In Mary's case, God moved her out of an abusive marriage and then launched her out into her vision. She saw her vision for the first time when she was already middle-aged. Mary started working on her vision in prayer and came to a Kingdom advice center, where God started to prophesy that He would be taking her forward into a new step of freedom.

There was an unexpected time of deliverance when she discovered a demon had been given authority over her life by her grandparents when she was a young child. The demon was dealt with in Jesus' name and within days Mary had launched out into a greater level of freedom in the prophetic and was starting to step out in the first stages of the practical outworking of her vision.

God increasingly deals with the specters of rejection and other issues of low self-esteem. He's raising places where these things can be dealt with confidentially and quickly, in the same way Jesus dealt with them. I have seen so often that when the time is right He will move it forward. God will allow a certain level of issues to remain inside of us until we are ready to be moved forward into a different level of promotion and breakout.

Where Am I? Assessing Progress and Charting What God Is Doing in My Life

In the process of getting to the other side of your Jordan, you will be using journaling, one of the activations we use in teaching the prophetic, and holding up your eight-point destiny locator as a plumb line for when you're going.

When we are on the right track with God and our vision, all should be going well. God gives the vision and then animates it with motivation, provision and energy. Unfortunately as we all know, sometimes **life gets tough**. Sometimes even when we are on track with God, stuff gets in the way and we find ourselves wallowing through treacle to move a single step.

We cry out to God for help and expect Him to remove the obstacles and help us through. But is this the right way forward? What if we are in fact not on the right track at all? What if our vision is not God-inspired, but our own very human desires are trying to force themselves to the fore?

In that case, God tries to get our attention and show us what He really wants for us; but it is possible to miss it for a season, and when we do God gradually reduces the flow of his Spirit to our vision.

He reduces the motivation, provision and energy to what we are doing and we start to flounder and cry out to our friends to support us in prayer. But that is little use when it is God Himself who has brought us to this state to get our attention.

So how can we tell the difference? How can we be sure that we are on the right track with our vision? How can we know when it is God, or when it is an attack and we have to stand up and fight for what God is holding out to us? One thing we know is that any true vision from God will be contested.

God has a hedgerow of protection around everyone of us. When we find setbacks in our calling however, we have to determine the source of the problem. The most common answer is that it is God's refining hand at work. God is putting us into a challenging situation to further train our hands for war, or to refine our character in some way. "Training for reigning" is the most common form of encounter with difficulties we have.

Most of the time when we think it is satan or other people attacking us, it is in fact God teaching us to work with adversity. It is God who allows people to go through a trial. If you think your difficulties are an attack upon your calling, you need to ask God why an attack is coming. Maybe He will say it's coming because of the doors opened into your life by family, church, relationships, etc. The other big factor to take into consideration is sin. Sin opens doorways for satan to enter.

God's Timing and Seasons

Which season are you in? A constant dialogue with God is needed to establish what time and season you are in and what is happening to cause the problem. Maybe God says He's allowing it, so you ask why and God says if you go down that route now it will lead to future difficulties.

Only God really knows the full repercussions of what we do and the decisions we make. If He turns off our flow, we must always seek His guidance about why. It is foolish to try and push through on your own, instead of seeking the Lord and working with Him in it.

I think there's another dimension, which is that God may be wanting to do some refining and he may be allowing seasons of being in the heat and in the cold to build character. If you're not getting grace and you can't get peace and you've worked through all these points as we've gone through them, I think the Lord might want to take what could be a snare out of your heart. All these things come back to hearing God.

Then there is the possibility that God is turning off your motivation and His provision because you have made a mistake about your calling. You need to go through the eight points again, and see if God has built a core competence in you for it.

Even in a situation where you are convinced that you are right and your friends are supporting you, if you are wrong, you will simply not progress with the calling you think you have. Your friends do not determine your destiny. Eventually you will have to get before God and ask Him what's happening. He will tell you what He thinks about it all and what to do from that point.

The Process of Vision

Sarah's vision started 20 years ago. She knows what it is like to keep a vision on the back burner while following the Lord and gradually watching the vision unfold. Her experience is of persevering. Her advice to all visionaries would be not to give up on it just because it doesn't happen straight away.

When Sarah started, she didn't have a vision. Sarah has lived in one place almost all of her married life, so she's in a different scenario from people who move about. Although Sarah is by birth one of England's top-drawer people, coming from generations of landowners, God gave her a heart for the land and for the people on one of the local council estates.

The estate is a microcosm of inner city problems and Sarah started to get involved with families there 20 years ago. She has a particular friend whom her church asked her to mentor. This friend came from a completely unchurched background and from a very different culture than Sarah, but Sarah found herself involved in her situation.

She was also asked by the health visitors and social workers to be a friend to some of the other families there. So she started working with kids and some of the people on the estate and getting to know what was happening. She was quite involved with it all and growing with God in the meantime. It was a time of getting to know God, and while she saw God working miracles, most of all she saw God's heart for the poor and needy.

In 1990 there was a movement, called Dawn 2000, to plant 2,000 churches by the dawn of the year 2000. When Sarah heard that, she prayed, "Oh Lord, let's plant a church on the estate, and develop a community center up there." That was when her vision really crystallized. Since that time, she has known God was saying plant a church on the estate. At the time it was an audacious prayer, but now, from this end of the spectrum, it sounds like quite a normal prayer.

One of the ways Sarah got her street credibility in the community was by becoming a dinner lady in the local primary school for three years. She worked on the playground and she was also a classroom assistant. She had wonderful opportunities to share the Lord on the playground and pray with the kids.

God was training her and she started running holiday clubs. Sarah is a visionary but not a strategist, so she knows she's reliant on God to give her His plans as she works with the vision. She had no idea how it was going to happen. Then one day, her vision died.

When the Vision Dies

She was in YWAM working with King's Kids. She had to do a presentation of what she wanted to see happen on the estate, and she knew as she was speaking it out that all the life had gone from her vision. The whole thing just went dead inside her. It was a time of grieving. For about four months the vision was dead.

Then her son said to her "Mum, do you still care about the people on the estate?" Sarah said she did. So he said, "If you were dying, would you regret that you hadn't carried on working with them?" It was then that it hit her. It was a defining moment in confirming the vision because she knew, deep in her spirit, that she wanted to do it.

It wasn't just something that was a good idea. It was the time that the seed of her vision germinated. The seed had been sown in her heart and it was alive and she had a passion for it, but only now did she know that if push really came to shove, whatever happened in life and whatever she would go through, she knew she wanted to do it. It was almost like a born-again experience for her. She knew that this was what God was calling her to, and wanted with all her will to be obedient to Him.

Then different things started to happen. She did a leadership course. She got passionate about cell churches and thought cell churches were going to be the answer. She kept talking to people about different models of church. It was an interesting time for her. She was experiencing different things and talking to people about a variety of church shapes. But she knew that none of it really quite fit with her estate.

Sarah's Little Hobby

Sarah and her husband bought a house on the estate about three years ago and that gave them a stake in the land. For Sarah, the vision is not just to see a church planted, but also to see it in the context of the land. She is called to work with local kids and their families, and sees them as the keys to healing the land. They are the evidence that shows you the land needs to be healed. As people see the kids' lives being turned around and being healed, they will know the land is being healed.

All the time it was like Sarah's little hobby to other people. Nobody was motivated to share it with her. People were too tied up with what they were doing to get on board Sarah's passion. They did not understand it. No church planted on the estate had ever survived and flourished. It was a dead zone. But Sarah prayed and people prayed with her. She walked the land in prayer and organized friends to pray. She kept praying God's will into being.

Kingdom Advice Center

Then Sarah came to the Kingdom advice center in the area. It was another defining moment for her. She knew the first night there that her ministry wasn't in the church, wasn't among Christians and wasn't in some organizational church, it was out there in the community and that's where her destiny was, that's where God had placed her.

That was her ministry and that was her church, these non-Christian kids from the estate. We started encouraging her in the vision. There were lots of prophetic words and God was really encouraging her. All at once the whole thing made sense to her.

Art Rocks

She started running "art rocks" a couple of years ago, which is a Friday night art youth club for eight- to fourteen-year-olds. They have been through a process with establishing that, as the kids have been wild at times and it has taken time for them to trust her.

Several of the children are excluded from school. There are kids in the same family where each child has a different father, or where there are parents on drugs. Most of the families have single mums. Part of the vision is also to give the kids opportunities to get training, to do what God has called them to do.

It will be like a "come-and-go" church. Come all you who are weary and heavy laden, and then, go and make disciples. They can go and make church wherever they are. There's a real sense of community between kids, as they have so many contacts and links with one another. Sarah can see it spreading and she's excited by what God's doing.

From having been very difficult, the kids now love coming and it is a safe place for them. There are no strict rules and regulations. Sarah's ethos is to bring the unconditional love of God to these kids. She won't exclude anyone and if things go wrong one day, they close down and everybody has to go home, even though it may be only one kid who misbehaved.

She refuses to exclude even one kid. There are some pretty wild moments. But she has found what happens is that they come back and say they are sorry. Very often purely on their own they feel very convicted about the things they have done wrong, rather than Sarah having to discipline them or inflict punishment on them. The whole thing is Holy Spirit-led.

Dropping in on the Vicar

Another funny thing is that they have started dropping in on the Anglican church Sarah attends. They all piled into the wooden pews and sat with her. It's a very traditional, old-fashioned church service so they were asking questions like, "What's this holy water stuff?" and "Why do you have bread and wine?"

They were completely ignored by the rest of the congregation. Sarah asked if they would like a drink and they said yes, so she said for them to come along and say that they were with her. On another occasion about 12 of them piled in during evensong.

There was a lay reader doing the service and he explained to them about the nunc dimmitis and other parts of the service. The kids kept interrupting the service to ask questions loudly, as they don't have any such inhibitions at all.

Time to Move

Sarah knows that now is the time to start the church. Christian International is preparing to commission Tim and Sarah to do it. She is planning to start very simply, probably just ten or fifteen minutes. It would have to be led by them, with Sarah steering operations. It has to be hands-off, allowing the people to explore and ask questions rather than her imposing stuff on them.

It is the joy of the Lord that is the mainstay of the operation. One day, in a vision, Jesus took Sarah's hand and they went round the estate visiting families and homes. Sometimes He would lead and other times Sarah would.

All the time she felt incredible joy. Then they went to a grassy patch in the middle of the estate and Jesus sat down and Sarah knew that this was His land and these were His people and that He was going to make His home there.

Strategy Is From God

As the time draws nearer for you to be practically engaged hands-on in the early stages of your call, it becomes even more important to seek guidance and direction from God. If you ask Him, God will give clear direction and strategy as to how to pray and how to implement things in practical terms.

All of us need to hear God's strategy. But it's not a question of abdicating our own responsibility, or failing to use the common sense God has given us. When God comes in with a strategy you will need all of your life experience to enable you to fulfill it. God's strategies are overwhelmingly better than our own because He sees the bigger picture. He imparts strategy and we come to Him and listen for every step of the way. It's all to do with living in close relationship with God.

Living in Relationship With God

Living in relationship with God is based on the same principles as all other relationships. For a relationship to be real and healthy, you need to spend time together. You need to communicate and tell each other the things that are worrying you, ask for advice, be there for the other person and listen to them and their hopes and dreams. So it is with us and God.

We need to spend time with Him, to confide our heart's desires to Him and to listen to Him telling us His hopes and dreams. We need to ask His advice for our problems and interact with Him at every level. We need to hear Him telling us He loves us, deeply, personally and intimately.

To be in full relationship with Him we need to spend time with Him. We need to learn to hear His voice, not just when He forcibly breaks into our attention and speaks, but also in the daily small ways of interacting throughout our lives.

No one would embark on a marriage relationship with a partner they could not speak to, or tell their hopes and desires to. No one would expect to spend a week with their partner without touching them or sitting in the same room with them. Yet so many of us do that with God. Because we don't know how to interact with Him, we fail to make any contact and just assume that because so many other Christians seem to treat God in that way, that it's normal.

It may be common, but it is not normal. Being passionate about our Lord who died for us is what is normal in His eyes, just as He is passionate about us. It's about walking close to the God who loves us and sitting daily with Him under His affirmation.

Intimacy

It is not for the fainthearted to seek to enter into such close relationship with God that they start to live out what they profess to believe. If all God's people in your village were passionate about the Lord and did what He asked them to do on a daily basis, it would change the life of that village.

Imagine if everyone understood God's calling of them and the purpose He created them for, and worked with Him under His anointing to fulfill that calling. There would be companies working for the good of the community, reaching out to the disadvantaged and needy. People would be talking and living the gospel.

Imagine being so close to God that you pray with power against corruption in your town and you tear down the strongholds that bring drugs and hopelessness to your city's families and children.

True obedience can only come from love, not from any other source, or it becomes prideful and tainted. Only love brings obedience and true servant-hood. Close relationship brings love, intimacy with the Lord, and personal joy and fulfillment.

Figure 2—Walking Out the Call

By the time we are actually embarking on the early stages of our vision, we will have had much freedom from foreign gods brought to us by the hand of the Lord and His grace and mercy. We will be flying with Him in the high places, in intimate relationship with Him. If you have reached this part of your vision and you haven't learned to fly with God, you are working in the dark.

At this point, in terms of the river of the Spirit, you are swimming. In terms of relationship with God, you are in the high places. In terms of your vision, you are only just beginning to set foot upon your destiny. It is a very exciting time.

Then we start to encounter things that most of us don't normally anticipate when we are walking with God. The first thing we encounter is that God comes in and circumcises us. We discover the fire of God upon us, but also discover a greater level of commitment and passion for Him as He circumcises our hearts.

Less exciting for most of us, though certainly no less significant in God's eyes, is the fact that He usually also comes in and circumcises our finances at this point. God provides the plans, purposes, motivation, energy and resources, and He carries the risk. So we do not need our own investments in this and we shouldn't worry about it.

Even if you are prepared for financial circumcision, it still comes as a shock. It is a time of challenge, but it is also a time of growing in faith, of increasing trust and of deepening commitment. It is a time of choice and a time when you either have to trust Him and walk forward with Him, or turn away and say that it is not for you. But if you do that, you walk away from your destiny.

Everyone's challenges are different and there will be some people for whom the circumcision will not be so visible financially. All the visionaries I have worked with have gone through a time when God

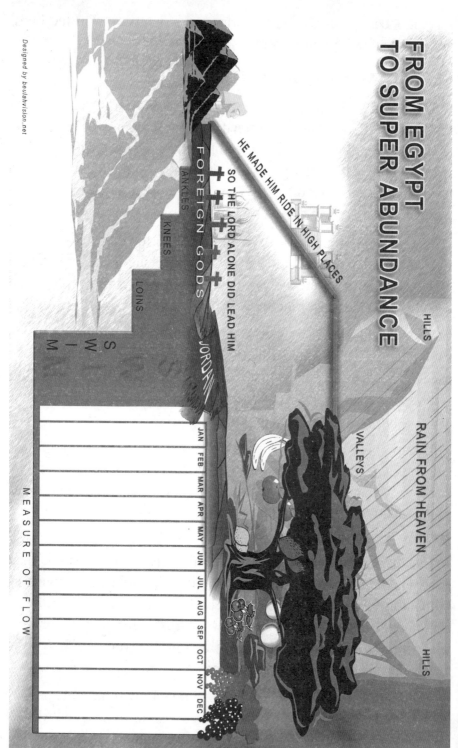

Figure 2 -Walking Out the Call

challenges them right where it hurts, as to whether they are going to walk His way or theirs.

Don't misunderstand me, I'm not saying God gives you poverty and I'm not saying God does not prosper His people, because He does. But there are times when He withdraws that from them in order to sharpen their minds, to increase their faith, and to fulfill some purpose to take them forward with Him.

He also prepares you for such a time. The Word assures us that He sends us nothing we cannot bear. Prosperity and abundance are on their way. As you walk into your destiny, your destiny will bring you prosperity and it will be filled with abundance.

As God has promised in Joshua 1:7-9,

Only be thou strong and very courageous, that thou mayest observe to do according to all the law, which Moses my servant commanded thee: turn not from it to the right hand or to the left, that thou mayest prosper whithersoever thou goest. This book of the law shall not depart out of thy mouth; but thou shalt meditate therein day and night, that thou mayest observe to do according to all that is written therein: for then thou shalt make thy way prosperous, and then thou shalt have good success. Have not I commanded thee? Be strong and of a good courage; be not afraid, neither be thou dismayed: for the LORD thy God is with thee whithersoever thou goest. (KJV)

The whole wealth of nations belongs to God. He can provide for us supernaturally in whatever way He chooses, and often the ways He chooses are quite unexpected. Often money comes to us in unexpected ways and from unexpected quarters. I sometimes think He delights in doing things differently from the way we expect.

We can't rely on our expectations. People who could help us out, don't; people who are perhaps in a worse position than we are, do. Contracts we'd never expected suddenly come our way, whereas the one we'd been banking on falls flat. It's all part of growing nearer to God. It's all part of walking closer and trusting deeper.

It's all part of the growing relationship and intimacy with the One who loves us so much, beyond measure, beyond time, beyond understanding. Until you have that insight into the love of God, you cannot hope to walk through this period of circumcision.

The manna of God's provision continues for a time until God gets you to the first point of wealth transfer from your land. Then the manna stops, just as when Joshua crossed into the Promised Land the manna ceased and the people ate from the land. Once they'd taken dominion and habitation, God showed them how to live off the land.

So it is with us, some sources of provision that God has provided and we had assumed were going to continue, suddenly stop. But we discover that even in the early stages of our vision, God is providing for us. Not in the way we had wanted, for the early wealth transfer usually falls short of abundance and we don't feel we've made it yet, but He is providing it.

This is a time when choices are difficult and in the natural we would choose to do things that are sensible and probably directly opposed to God's plan for us, so it is essential that we grasp hold of His leading during this exciting transition, this adventure into our destiny. It is a great adventure of discovery, led daily by the Lord.

Many Spheres Make a Destiny

As discussed in Chapter 3, each one of us is like an individual sphere of function as we walk out our destiny. Our destiny has a purpose for God. Our destiny may be comprised not of one sphere, but of many spheres. Although our calling in God remains the same, our vision grows.

We may be influencing other people and our destiny will have links to other peoples' spheres. We don't want to see ourselves as just one single sphere of function, rather each of the activities God is calling us into is a single sphere, so our destiny is most likely to be comprised of several different spheres all interacting together. But we are connected in different ways.

I want to teach workplace and marketplace ministers in every nation to hear the voice of God. So how am I going to do this? Through the media! I started a prophetic business network and God made a way for me to go from governance ministries to Christian International, up on Dr. Hamon's and Sharon Stone's platform so that I come under that anointing He put on those organizations, which helps me demonstrate, duplicate and multiply it.

God had me trained in the God Channel, the first Christian channel in Europe, then He put me in the position to be heading up Trinity Broadcasting Corporation in Europe, so I'm sowing into media organizations and I am going to be in a position where I can release the training of the prophetic through manuals, publishing and television. All of these things God orchestrated, as I was faithful during my first stage of ministry.

Then He gives me a Kingdom advice center to start. Then He gives me more Kingdom advice centers to start. He prophesied to me lately that the supernova is showering, getting brighter and getting bigger, representing more weight on the Word and more acceptability in more areas.

That helps me know I'm on track of getting from nowhere to raise up workplace and marketplace ministers in every nation who can hear God's voice, and that God is going to open up more people groups to me. He has opened up a people group through Rich Marshall and He opened up a people group through Stewart Lindsell and Martin Scott.

He spoke into my watchman sphere. I didn't know how the watchman sphere fit, so I just drew it as a sphere and then started to wait, actively wait and ask and look, and I started to get prophetic words about watchmen. God brought Martha Lucia, an international watchman, into my sphere. You need to watch how God adds things to your various spheres.

That's how you find you're on track. You have your basic plan laid out and you're looking for either prophetic words, words from God, what other people see in your life or new skills. He might ask you to learn Spanish and then you'll find someone will prophesy you're going to be speaking to Spanish nations, or when you're journaling with God, He'll mention "You'll be going to Spain next year." He'll add bits to all your coordinates. He'll go around each of these areas motivating people to encourage you to be on line and He'll put a block on you if you go off line.

Focusing on Your Mission

My whole life is focused on my mission. If I'm given opportunities that are not working according to my mission statement I don't do them. That's how I keep focused. But primarily I stay on course by being obedient to what God's telling me to do today. Not always of course, but I couldn't go on very long without asking how I am doing.

Our vision is not straightforward and there are many interactions we must learn to flow with and understand so we will need God's help to guide us in how to operate. You need God's guiding, otherwise you will do it your own way and fulfill only part of the destiny you could have had.

Supernatural Fruit

We should expect that God will give us supernatural fruit every month once we are on course and flowing with Him. Are we planning for supernatural fruit every month, are we praying for it? Are we walking in the fullness of the flow? How do we increase the rain upon our land?

Initially, particularly during the time of the circumcision and the early wealth transfer, when you know God is providing but it's not enough for you to feel as if you've made it, it's all too easy to get into survival mode. But we have to keep our eyes on the promises of God and remember that His promise to each one of us is abundance and that we should be prepared for His supernatural fruit to flow every month. The early time is a time to stand on what God has said to us. It is the early times that will set us up for the way we are to go.

God will show you how to increase the measure of rain upon your land if you ask Him. He will show you what the specific measures are that you need to take. One universal key however is intimacy with Him. **The closer you are to Him, the greater the abundance in every area of your life**. Prayer is another universal key. It moves the hand of God and brings further revelation and intimacy.

The time of circumcision is incredibly important. If you study the time of the circumcision at Gilgal, you will see it is the time God rolls away the reproach of Egypt. It is a time of greater commitment. Gilgal was a very significant place in biblical history. People kept returning to it. It is the place where the ark remained while Joshua conquered the land until it was moved to Shiloh, another significant place in history.

The measure of abundance is not the issue. The measure will vary according to how may of your spheres are working at any one time. It will also vary as to where you are at walking out your destiny. And it will vary according to what your destiny is. So the measure is different for everybody. One couple that has been through much refining and circumcision is Mike and Lelonnie. They are Canadian, currently living in the U.K., but in the process of moving to America. Theirs is a worldwide vision.

Called for Children

Lelonnie has known since she was a child that she was called by God for His end-time harvest, but it was only when she and Mike got married that they realized they were to work with children. God called them right from the beginning of the marriage.

They spent the next 20 years working together with children in churches. No status, no authority, no position, just working with children. It became an integral part of their vision and their lives as God worked in them to deepen their heart and passion for children. They did not realize there was a pattern, or a wider purpose, they just faithfully did what God was asking day-by-day.

Twenty years later, Lelonnie had a vision from Heaven when God commissioned her and called her to "carry" the children of the world in prayer. At the 1997 revival meetings in London, God was again moving in them and putting deep things in their hearts.

That season had a giant impact on them as they found, individually and as a family, the presence of Jesus in deeper and more intense ways than they had known before. It was then they first began to receive prophetic words about their vision.

The vision sovereignly came by God, but it was described and given shape by the prophetic words they received. It only began to dawn on them that they were a family for the nations, for example, when it was prophesied over them. As they further yielded everything to God, He began to shape it inside of them.

Often when you get a prophetic word you don't understand what it means or get its full significance at that time. Mike and Lelonnie know they don't fully understand the far reaches of the vision even now, but Lelonnie admits the prophetic has had incredible impact on their lives.

You can't make a prophetic word happen, but you can say yes to the Lord and you can yield to God so He can prepare your life to cope with the prophecy, and you can call it in. That's what Mike and Lelonnie have been doing all these years and intercession has played a significant part.

Confirmation Always Comes

The next step was that over the next five years, God began to confirm the prophetic words they had received. He gave them more prophetic words and He confirmed the existing prophetic words. He began to give them divine appointments, connections and miracle meetings.

They had prophecies from all over the world. On one occasion, Lelonnie was in a meeting praying, when suddenly the word of the Lord came to her, saying "take the fragrance of Jesus to the children of the nations." A minute later, the leader of the meeting put her hand on Lelonnie's back and said, "Take the fragrance of Jesus to the children of the nations."

Repeatedly, they received confirmations that were word for word. There have been dozens of examples of divine connections. Someone e-mailed Lelonnie about a lady in Australia who led children's prayer. Lelonnie was so excited she carried the letter around with her for ten days.

Then she found herself in a room with the same lady without knowing who she was. God told her to speak to her. They both knew there was a real God-connection being made when Lelonnie pulled out her tattered e-mail and asked her if she knew the person and she said it was her! That's the kind of divine connections they have had time after time.

They came to the Kingdom advice center in Guildford, England and the words brought were incredibly confirming. Lelonnie says they were miracle words to them, where God actually gave people who knew nothing about them, word for word, the words He had spoken to them over the years.

Refining, Refining, Refining

Lelonnie says that for many years she wallowed in false humility, saying "how can I do this, I'm not qualified," and unbelief, "maybe I'm dreaming and the Lord isn't really asking me to carry these things."

Then the Lord said "Enough!" very, very strongly, through a prophetic word to her. He said He had set a glorious field before her, that she must receive it by faith, and He had had enough of her unbelief. So she had to simply choose to believe God at His word, no matter what it felt like. Lelonnie and Mike carry the vision together, as there is a real partnership in the midst of their different gifts and abilities.

In the last three years as the vision has been shaped, there has been a refining process. It has come in stages. First it was learning to walk by faith through all sorts of things. Their financial situation was the biggest hardship. They had to give up their home in order to walk in the early stages of the vision. Time and time again God has stretched them to the breaking point, where they did not think they could live another day without provision or they would see financial ruin. It has stretched their faith, but they decided to embrace what God was doing.

The second part of the refining process was dying to self. John the Baptist said, "I may decrease that He may increase." That has been a reality in Mike and Lelonnie's lives. In the past few years they have had to learn a different way of living. It's easy to live sweetly as a Christian when everything is going well, but it's not so easy to live that way when you are being betrayed, treated badly and being hurt.

But the Lord very clearly said to them over and over again that they were to choose to instantly forgive. In those times the Lord has challenged them to die to themselves and live in love. Their rights had to go, their pride had to go and losing face had to be lived with.

When God comes in like this you have to literally die, die, die. It's as if you have no rights. Humble yourselves before God and don't care what others think of you. Once you make that choice, the Lord comes in and helps you to live that way. Part of it is that if the Lord gives you a giant vision, you have to be made into a vessel to carry that vision. God refines us all through the difficulties and life experiences we have to go through.

Kansas City

Today the vision has reached the point that they both know God has called them for the rest of their lives. Mike has been called as a forerunner to prepare the way for the coming of the Lord. The Lord has called the family to Kansas City for a season, to the International House of Prayer, Mike Bickle's center of worship and prayer.

Together, they are called to see all children of all nations reached with the gospel, rescued in the midst of dire circumstances and released to become radical followers of Jesus. Lelonnie says, "This is the Lord's vision, it is what He wants to do and we serve Him in it, not because He needs us but because He is so awesomely gracious and allows us to partner with Him. We are called to partner in humility with countless others the Lord connects us with around the globe as He sovereignly orchestrates the reaching, rescuing and releasing of these children."

God has given them three vehicles to achieve this aim. The first is prayer. They believe it is God's "kairos" time to develop a children's prayer network across nations and tap into the incredible faith of children. Children believe God at His word and when they pray, they believe He will make a difference. They have collected dozens of stories from across the world which prove that even one praying child can influence the destiny of a nation.

The second vehicle is media. They plan to use television, books and resources to facilitate the release of artists, authors and musicians. The third vehicle is partnering with business, forging a living relationship between businesses and children. Offering businesses the opportunity to invest in God's end-time purposes, in world revival and in emerging generations.

Mike and Lelonnie both know that the most important thing in their lives is the presence of Jesus. Lelonnie told me, "If you are in the presence of Jesus, what took you six weeks to accomplish will take you six days. I cannot emphasize it enough. It is guaranteed you will find your vision if you go into the throne room. As God gives you a vision He helps you to work out that vision. Step-by-step God will tell you how to walk out your vision. It is very important that you don't do anything unless He has said to do it. You don't connect until he says to connect. You need to be in a place where you are dependent. Wait until there is faith or a sense of the word of the Lord saying to do it."

Lelonnie added, "We always knew God could give big visions, but we struggled because we wondered if we were hearing right. We questioned who were we to carry such a vision, but eventually we just had to let go of all that strong sense of being unqualified. Someone very wise said to us: 'Praise God for your weakness, the weaker you are the more you qualify for His grace and mercy; yes, you are unable but He lives in you, and He is utterly able.' So now when the vision still overwhelms us at times, we rest in nothing less than the truth that Jesus is able.

Future and Fulfillment

So how does destiny and the fulfillment of purpose relate to the end-time Church? My understanding from the Lord is that He has purposed our membership ministry from the beginning of time. Given our membership ministry in His Body, whether it's as journalist, doctor, pulpit minister, electricity worker, pilot or whatever, He has prepared a purpose and destiny for us.

He is preparing His Body to be ready for Him to come back. For His Body to be ready He has to get them into their place of destiny and the process of achieving their destination. They have to understand that it isn't just an unconnected thing, but that the place of their destiny is in the membership of His Body.

My overall understanding of how He wanted His Body to come together and function is covered in 1 Corinthians 12:1-28. I believe God through the Holy Spirit is moving us along toward our destiny, giving us the freedom to move into new levels so we can fulfill our part of what He's called us to do in His functioning Body.

He's perfecting us and getting us to a place where we can be seen without spot or wrinkle. He is also getting us delivered and bringing us to a level of freedom, while He is allowing a level of purification so that His whole body is prepared to lose everything to keep that eternal love with the Lord.

I see Him wooing each of the elements and parts of the Body, the one universal, many-membered, corporate Body of Christ. He is wooing every one of those many members to get them to the stage where they have such a foundation of love for Him that no matter what evil is loosed around them that they would still make a choice for Him.

Each of these steps that the Lord takes us through on the road to our destiny, each of these promotions, each of these levels of being given greater freedom, is to get us to the place where no matter what would be thrown at us, nothing would compensate for losing that love relationship with Jesus, that sweet communion, that walking and talking friendship, that intimacy with our God.

For those who are moving toward their destiny in the love of God and in relationship with the Lord, they will navigate and negotiate the persecution and the challenges of what is to come. The choices that they are given and the temptations that they are presented will simply not compare to their love and their choice to spend eternity with God.

CHAPTER 8

Fashioning a Living Stone

Four Million Dollars Lost

For many people, a personal relationship with God starts with thinking that God has chosen them because they have something to give, such as their wealth or their competence. People get excited about what they can do for God. Because the world has told us we are valued by what we can give and contribute, we get excited about being able to contribute and give to God.

In worldly terms, we may be valued by our wealth and talent but such values are set by criteria that do not cut any ice with Jesus. That's because Jesus came to serve and to give and to do both sides of the deal. The process of entering a relationship with the Lord involves Him coming to remove all our performance criteria, all the acceptance hurdles we have built up and think we need to enter into a relationship with Almighty God.

In my own walk with God, I was born again at a time when I had achieved all my goals. I was comparatively wealthy, as I was a millionaire with a net worth of $4 million or £2.5 million sterling. I had a millionaire's apartment on the Thames, a Bentley, a yacht and my Rolex—all signs of having achieved worldly success. My walk with Jesus actually started because those things never filled the hole in my soul. When I entered my relationship with the Lord, I would talk to Him about the things I could do and the things I had.

I'd talk about how I could make them available to Him. It was a massive shock to my system to discover Jesus had no need of my resources; He had no need of my success. In fact He could and would deliver not only His part of the salvation deal, but also my part of the contract if I would simply be obedient to Him. It took a while to come to terms with that.

So after various times of getting into difficult situations as the result of my own poor decisions, where I couldn't hear His voice or discern His will for my life, I continued going the way I always had and managed to lose the $4 million. Even as I was losing it, I continued saying to the Lord, "Don't you understand how useful this $4 million could be for your Kingdom?" But it did not cut the ice! It was as if the Lord said, "What I need is your heart. What I need is a one-to-one relationship. What I need is your yieldedness to Me. You need to praise and worship Me and to glorify My name."

Filling the Hole in Me

During my walk with the Lord over the course of 17 years to date, I've come to understand that the Lord did both parts of the deal and as He showed me the results of obedience and yieldedness to His hand, I began to find the hole in me that could not be filled by millions of dollars was being filled simply by His Person.

As He began to fill the void in me, joy would fill my being. Energy filled the hole, plans and purpose filled the hole, resources filled the hole. And it was as those things began to fill the void, that I began to see praise and worship and the glorifying of Jesus birthed out of a level of love that He had placed inside me.

It was birthed out of a knowledge of Him performing my part of the contract even when I had been totally inadequate time after time. It was a result of Him continuing to fill the void inside me with joy and energy and purpose and resources despite my shortcomings. Worship just became a natural thing to express how I felt about Him doing that. It led me into a place where after He loved me, tears would just stream down my face as all of the things happening in my heart caused all else to pale in significance.

That was the honeymoon period for me, that time in the relationship when God does everything for you. That was the period of financial miracle after financial miracle. God took my finances, which had gone from $4 million positive to £250,000 sterling negative, and worked that out for me. He carried me through lawsuits that were brought erroneously and fraudulently, lawsuits that could have ended up with me getting a £50,000 fine, that by that time I had no means to cover, and with me going to prison for two years.

I even came to the place where I had talked to my wife and two daughters about the likelihood that prison was the next step because I couldn't afford to pay the fine. I couldn't even afford to pay a barrister to argue my case for me. I tried to speak for myself but the judge stopped me since I was losing badly to the other barrister as a result of my ignorance of the processes of law in the high court. But God came through for me. One day He spoke to me about Daniel going into the lions den, and the Scripture (Daniel 6:22) where the next day the king ran out to see if Daniel was still alive. He told me that against the odds I would be delivered. Within two weeks my lawyer rang up and said it had just been confirmed that the case against me had been thrown out of court (after 7 years) and that all my costs would be paid by the other side. I was in the lions den but God stopped them from touching me.

In the Trenches

The next stage is when the Lord says, "So far I've done everything for you, both sides of the deal; and I'm going to continue to do both sides of the deal, but you're going to have to do a greater part. It is My plan that having paid the fullness of the price, there comes a time when you move from the milk to eat strong meat and you begin to become mature. Because when I came to take away all the power of the enemy, even down to the power of death, I took away the keys from the enemy.

And I want you to enforce My victory in all circumstances, in trials that you walk through, and in the things I orchestrate and allow for your training to produce a godly character."

I'm telling you though, that if you go through things as I went through them, you begin to feel like cannon fodder for the Lord's purposes. I knew enough to want to do what He wanted. I knew enough to want to be yielded to Him. But my concept of God at that time and in those circumstances was that I was in a battle that was horrible and I knew I had to be there, but I didn't want to be there. I had to have my hard hat on and dodge the bombs as they came, and every time the Lord said do this and do the other, I would go and do it.

I could praise and worship corporately, but I allowed the lie of the enemy to come in and steal my personal relationship with the Lord for about four years between 1997 and 2001. It was because I misunderstood the maturing process. The Lord was working on my character and He was showing me the depth of the foundations He had put in me to enforce His victory in every situation and circumstance. And He was showing me that there was an open heaven in the midst of those situations when I saw myself as just having my hard hat on in the trench and dodging the bullets. If only I could appropriate that open heaven with an understanding of spiritual laws.

Throughout those four years of events that would come to have massive significance in the work that I was involved in and the people I was working with, I always knew that God would come and rescue me in the end. I'd envision Him coming in on His white horse on the 11th hour, 59th minute, and 59th second, and He would make everything all right. But in the midst of that turmoil I had moved to a place where I could not praise or worship or glorify Him, for I could only remember the pain of being in the trenches.

Healed by a Street Preacher

At the end of the four years, in His mercy, the Lord ministered to me through a street preacher. I went into that place that I have experienced with the Lord before, where He immobilized my body and did what I call supernatural surgery with me as I was lying on the floor. And he took me through the paradigm shift that I was unable to grasp for myself, where I had been unable to see the truth in His Word about all those times of oppression I had experienced.

In the process, He showed me that His only intention during those times when I used to feel abused was that I would understand in the midst of persecution that there is an open heaven. Just as Stephen, in the midst of being stoned and persecuted, could see Jesus supernaturally in Heaven, so He showed me that the Lord supernaturally would become our anesthetist during trials and attacks. He showed me that He would anaesthetize all of the wounds, all of the tribulation, all of the bruises, all of the pain, all of the cuts, all of the swipes, all of the betrayal, and all of the abuse that could be dealt out.

He showed me that if we could only worship and praise Him and glorify His name during those difficult moments, that we would have an open heaven. And with that open heaven would come the presence of the Healer who would come and supernaturally take away all of that natural pain, all of that abuse and all of that stuff that makes one feel like cannon fodder.

It is our yieldedness in those situations and being able to call forth an open heaven that brings His majesty into the situation, that brings His authority into the situation, that brings His love into the situation. Those things anaesthetize our soul. His presence makes every wound, every hurt, every ungodly belief, every demonic oppression, be washed away. It anaesthetizes the effects on the soul. It comes like a spiritual eraser that erases our pain and wounds and makes us ready for the next battle.

So as we move on in our personal walk with the Lord, we move through that phase and begin to enjoy and relish the battle. Because in the midst of those things, when we are taught to wield the sword of the Spirit, when we are taught that we have been given His power and authority, then we begin to see that He has given us a set of tools and a set of patterns based on principles that can bring heaven to earth at that moment. We can bring the supernatural to work at that moment, and that can bring the Healer, the anesthetist for our soul, into those situations, enabling us to enforce His victory in every situation.

Yielding, Yielding, Yielding

With the increasing knowledge and understanding that He releases to us comes a responsibility on our part, if we have a yieldedness to His plans, and are willing to work out His strategies in the way He has asked us to. It is in many of those situations where the enemy deceives us and our soul rises up and says I can't do this and I won't do this and I'm ticked off, and all the other things that our moaning brings forth. God graciously leaves us in that position until we can stand up in maturity and put on His armor, so that we can go and follow the course that He has set for us.

In that process, we call down heaven on earth and as He releases angels to help, we get an open heaven. It is then that we see Him come and move in those situations we no longer look at mournfully and what we see is the majesty of our God so our hearts rise up to glorify and worship Him. The more that happens, the more His authority comes and the more His glory comes. He taught that everything we need to fulfill our walk with him, everything we need to achieve what He has given us to do, is in His glory. But if we can't bring the glory down, if we can't move in the glory, if we can't experience an open heaven, we can't achieve those things.

No matter where you are, even if you've had all that you own stripped from you, leaving you with mounds of debt, no matter what your situation is, this personal relationship with Jesus that I've spoken of has come to set you free from it. It has come to give you liberty.

There will be a part where God will do it all and you will just be in awe of Him. But there will come a time when He will want to build godly character in you and allow you to walk through difficult situations so you can learn to be an overcomer in every situation.

As you build that character and progress through those steps of growth you then get to the stage that you begin to relish a battle, because you relish being that far out of the boat, so to speak. You know that as you lift your hands in praise and worship, as you lift your voice to call for His answers, strength and resources, you begin to see an open heaven.

It is because you know that your personal relationship, together with the knowledge and understanding of the tools He's given you, is able to bring the glory of God into your situation, which anaesthetizes your soul in the midst of persecution. It is able to bring the miraculous provision of God that is superabundantly more than you could ever imagine.

Relationship with God is not simply a matter of "being saved," as so many people seem to think. That's just the start. After that there is the growing, increasingly intimate relationship that develops as we learn to hunger after His person and seek Him out at all costs.

There are several areas in which we can see the growth of our relationship with the Lord: in conversational relationship, in the refining of our character and personal holiness, and in the place of intimate communing, that place where there is no person or thing that can keep us from enjoying His presence and sinking before Him with a heart poured out in adoration.

Listening to God

For the first three years of my Christian walk I had no teaching and no understanding of a personal relationship with the Lord. In my fourth year I had my first recognizable touch of the Holy Spirit, although with no framework or context. Certainly at that point I had no understanding that the Lord wanted a communicative type of relationship. But by 1992, after getting saved in December 1988, I began to understand that the Holy Spirit could be seen moving on people, could be heard through people, could be communicated with and could be spoken to, through my experience in Mike Price's church at Woodgate in Birmingham.

We had about four years of foundation building in that local church setting with a particular focus on learning to communicate with the Holy Spirit. This involved working through the school of the Spirit and watching the interaction of people and realizing that you could be trained to work with the Holy Spirit and even to see Him come upon people. Although the Lord opened visions and dreams to us in 1995 and 1996, it wasn't until 1997 that He put Pauline and I in a position where we could get proper training on how to activate prophecy in the world today.

In a concentrated period of one year, Dr. Sharon Stone coached and mentored Pauline and I in the prophetic, using Christian International prophetic training materials and training classes. It was a safe church environment where you could learn to hear the voice of God for yourself, but more importantly to hear the Lord's voice for other people.

It is when you can hear the voice of God for other people that not only can you exhort, comfort and encourage other Christians, you can also reach into the heart of those who do not know Jesus yet. We call that prophetic evangelism. It becomes a very powerful tool for letting people know that God is a communicator and that He wants to talk to them. To say, "this is what He has told me about you," lets that person know that God knows them and is interested in them, even though they have no relationship with Him.

Entering Into Dialogue

As we developed spiritually that year, there began to be an added dimension to our walk with the Lord where increasingly we could learn to discern His voice. There had been times through 1994 and 1995 when I began to sense God coming in a vision and a dream or giving me specific direction, like when He told me not to work for a week, but to read my Bible and He would show me what He could do. But by 1997 I had begun to see that it was possible to have a continual dialogue with the Lord.

Many people are used to hearing the Lord in a local church setting, but only a few are expecting God to speak to them in a work setting. Yet that can be dramatically increased by some concentrated time and focus on hearing the voice of God in the workplace. My own experience was that the more I entered into communication with God, the more our personal relationship developed.

Everyone who embarks upon this journey in the workplace is going to have to come to the place of hearing God in their particular area of ability, as it is sometimes difficult to know whether it is our natural competency or God that is speaking. I have found that the Lord is keen to come and confirm what He is saying in the areas of business or work.

For example, in the areas of organizational change and of consultancy, which were my areas of natural competency, the Lord would actually give me a tingling sensation on my tongue, like after getting an injection at the dentist, to show me when He was speaking through me. I have another testimony that when the Lord was encouraging a minister to step out and speak God's heart to people in a department store that he would feel a little kick in his stomach like a baby would kick inside the womb.

The Lord has various ways of encouraging our understanding that it is Him speaking with us, but it only lasts for a limited time. We get to the point when the Lord won't do that anymore. He actually said to me, "Son, you asked me to confirm something I just told you. How many conversations do you have with people during the day where you ask them to confirm what they've just said to you? You never do, do you? So why are you asking Me to confirm what I've said? I want people to be able to hear My voice and act on My voice."

I am now at the stage in my journaling with the Lord and in my conversations with the Lord that if I hear Him give me strategy and give me tactics, I move out on it. It goes right at the core of trust; it is a matter of believing that we hear the voice of God. But it also keeps us in the place of pressing into Him so closely that out of all the thoughts that go through our head, we can hear the voice of God as He enters every element of our working day.

We are reaching the time when God will no longer be confirming endlessly what He has said to us, for He'll be expecting to have a conversation with us and to confirm in that conversation that we've understood what He's said and will move on what He's said.

God's Special People

This type of relationship is not for a small group of people—it is for every saint in the army of the Lord. I asked God about this end-time army and He said, "My army is an extension of Me throughout every element of life: home, work, leisure, government and education. This army is not recognized by its uniform, it is recognized by its spirit, which connects it to My Spirit. It is made up of those that call Me Lord and do what I ask them."

The Lord also talked to me about training for this army: "There is no natural or worldly hierarchy, but rather it is the measure of their yieldedness, the degree of lordship over every element of their life. Those that allow themselves to be fashioned by My training programs, My battle preparation, My spiritual assault courses, these are the ones that have learned to hear My voice. They have learned that their destiny is in their membership position in My body, My army."

God even explained to me about the leadership of this army: "There are 'five star generals' that have their membership ministry in My army who are secretaries, cleaners, salesmen, homemakers, school teachers, grandparents, retired senior citizens, policemen and firemen, all who have yielded to My hand and do what I ask. They call Me Lord and do what I say. They can be recognized with spiritual eyes and be heard with spiritual ears."

As the Lord spoke to me about this army, he highlighted three dimensions to me: "The first dimension is authority that comes from yieldedness to My hand and grows as people grow through the trials they face. The second dimension is the situation people are speaking into, as there are different authorities for different situations even when I work through the same person. The third dimension is people's positional authority in My body, which is the authority that goes with position. This is not conferred by title or by natural hierarchy, but by the weight of authority I put on what they say and do in their functional position in the Body.

A homemaker can carry more weight of authority than a government minister—through My authority they can change laws in nations. This new day in My army and body is not the sight of parading power as the world has seen when governments of old paraded their numerical and technological power, but rather they are invisible in their numerical and spiritual technology—unless you have eyes to see and ears to hear."

The Lord reiterated, "You won't see that parade of My power unless you have ears to hear and eyes to see. It is not man that promotes in this army, it is not man that posts the individual in this army to duty. It is not man who determines how far an individual in this army can go. It is not man who organizes and sets up brigades and platoons or groups of individuals in this army. This army is organized by My Son, this army is put in position through the Holy Spirit. This army is connected and marshaled and sent by My Son."

Be encouraged, for God is moving. He is calling all of His people into their places of fulfillment in these days. Some of us have waited for years to know what our calling is while some are still children yet know who they are to be in Him. Times are changing and God is on the move in a new way. Open your eyes to see where He is going—and then make sure you're out there running with Him.

It doesn't matter who you are or where you've been. He is reaching out His arms to you and calling you to Him. Understand this: He may convict us, but He never condemns us. All He wants is to see us fulfilled in His purpose for us. So if you're one of Jesus' recruits, then get ready, for He is calling to you. He is holding out position, power and authority to you. Jesus is calling us all into our places.

CONTACT THE AUTHOR

Richard Fleming

Brookmans Park Teleport
Great North Road
Hatfield
Hertfordshire
AL9 6NE
United Kingdom

Tel. +44 (0) 1707 622699
E-mail: admin@workplaceministers.com

Website:
www.workplaceministers.com

Additional copies of this book and
other book titles from
DESTINY IMAGE EUROPE
are available at your local bookstore.

We are adding new titles every month!

To view our complete catalog on-line, visit us at:

www.eurodestinyimage.com

Send a request for a catalog to:

Via Acquacorrente, 6
65123 - Pescara - ITALY
Tel. +39 085 4716623 - Fax +39 085 4716622

* * * * * * * * * * * * * * * * * *

Are you an author?

Do you have a "today" God-given message?

CONTACT US

We will be happy to review your
manuscript for a possible publishing:

publisher@eurodestinyimage.com